THE POWER OF A PRAYER SUMMIT

Infecting the Affections through
Extraordinary Prayer in the Local Church

CONNIE ACKER

The Power of a Prayer Summit: Infecting the Affections through Extraordinary Prayer in the Local Church
© 2013 by Connie Acker / Strategic Renewal International

All rights reserved. No part of this publication may be reproduced in any form without written permission from Connie Acker / Strategic Renewal International.

Strategic Renewal
P.O. Box 365
Forest, VA 24551
Strategicrenewal.com

ISBN 978-0-9816090-3-4

Contents

PART 1: PRAYER SUMMIT VISIONS
Prayer Summit Beginnings 11
How a Prayer Summit Changed My Life 15
Stories of Personal Transformation 19
What is a Local Church Prayer Summit? 23
Benefits of the Local Church Prayer Summit for the Participant 27
Benefits of the Local Church Prayer Summit for the Pastor 35

PART 2: PLANNING THE SUMMIT
The Keys to a Successful Local Church Prayer Summit 45
Key People 49
Policies, Procedures, and First Things 55
The Summit Committee 63
Committee Job Descriptions 69

PART 3: PREPARING FOR THE SUMMIT
Preparing the Congregation 79
Facilitator Preparation 83
Preparation of the Summit Site 87

PART 4: CONVENING THE SUMMIT
Leading the Large Combined Group 93
Leading the Small Group 99
Communion 103
The Last Session and Afterward 109

Dedication

To my pastor, good friend, teacher and "adopted son," Daniel Henderson, who not only shared his prayer visions, but also infected me with his passion for worship-based prayer that seeks God's face. And for allowing me to minister with him as his visions of corporate prayer, based in worship, became a reality in the All Church Prayer Summits at Arcade Church.

And to the many brothers and sisters (100 +) who served willingly and sacrificially on the Summit Planning Committees and as facilitators at the Prayer Summits (You know who you are!). Without each of your contributions over the 10+ years that we served together, learned together, and grew together, this book could not have been written. So please accept my heartfelt thanks and appreciation and once more join me in praying for God's impact and renewal in the lives of the pastors and church leaders, who will read this book, as we did so often at "our" All Church Prayer Summits.

Foreword

Prayer Summits are a powerful and practical demonstration of the sufficiency of the word of God, the Spirit of God and the people of God. I believe every congregation can experience genuine transformation through the Prayer Summit model – and they should! Too much is at stake for the spiritual health of individual believers, for the renewal of the church and the glorious demonstration of Christ to a lost world for us not to give our very best to become a house of prayer for all nations.

My experience is that a Prayer Summit, when properly understood and effectively led, is an experience of Christianity in its purest form. These multi-day spiritual retreats are not about our common focus on programming, personalities or performance. Rather, they are an amazingly New Testament taste of Scripture-fed, Spirit-led, worship-based prayer. They will change the way you and your congregation pray for your good and His glory.

I've had the amazing privilege of leading Prayer Summits of all kinds and sizes. Some have been national Prayer Summits, attracting leaders from all across North America. Others have been regional summits, comprised of believers from dozens of churches. Still others have been exclusively for pastors in a particular metropolitan area. By far, my favorite Prayer Summits are local-church oriented summits where believers from the same congregation commit to give the Lord their undivided attention for an extended period of time. The Spirit produces a level of unity, transparency, commonality and ongoing relationship that is truly Heaven-sent.

In this book, you will come to understand the life-changing dynamic of a local church Prayer Summit. Connie Acker is an unusually gifted organizer and heart-felt communicator. I would not have been able to conduct many of the Summits I've enjoyed without her excellent administrative contribution and spiritual insight.

This book is an invaluable resource for any pastor and congregation desiring to take the bold and Christ-honoring step to experience the power of a Prayer Summit. My prayer is that you will be inspired and informed to implement the Prayer Summit model. My experience has proven that it will be a powerful force in teaching you to pray more effectively and a tool in the hands of Christ to restore His manifest presence among His people.

Daniel Henderson
President, Strategic Renewal

PART I

Prayer Summit Visions

Chapter 1
Prayer Summit Beginnings

We know we need to pray. God said so. Our souls cry out for a deeper connection with our Creator.

So why is it that the term "Prayer Summit" can project a negative image for some people? Perhaps it's because the term has a tendency to bring visions from childhood experiences of old-fashioned, prolonged prayer meetings. As a result, our perception of a Prayer Summit is a devotional service of people who pray long, wordy, and boring requests to God.

The word "summit" is scary because it conveys something over the top, something of a high degree or state. If this expresses your concerns or thoughts, let me assure you that the Prayer Summit experiences described in this book are something entirely different. A Prayer Summit is generally held over three and one-half days and is unlike a conference or a retreat.

Generally, a conference has keynote speakers and workshops conducted by those considered to be experts. The goal is to send the participants home more knowledgeable and better prepared by the topics covered. A retreat focuses on a pre-planned agenda, speakers, and often workshops designed to motivate, energize, and refresh the participants.

A Prayer Summit is an exciting encounter with God Himself. It's an experience that has the potential to change you, your family, your church, and your community. There are no agendas, speakers, workshops, or expert teachers. There is only one goal – to seek God's face.[1] Returning from his first Prayer Summit, one man put it this way:

> *I have listened to hundreds of sermons and attended many Christian seminars, conferences, and retreats. None of them made a lasting impression on me. I attended one church Prayer Summit and met the great I AM; my life changed forever.*

The concept of a Prayer Summit was promoted in 1989 by Dr. Joseph Aldrich, national evangelical leader and former president of Multnomah University Bible Seminar located in Portland, Oregon. The idea grew out of a desire for unity among pastors and church leaders. The original concept was an intense prayer gathering of pastors from many different denominations that would experience the renewing touch of God because of an extended time of effective and fervent prayer together.

When they returned home, the pastors hoped their experience of personal renewal and restoration would be a catalyst for reconciliation and unity among the various denominations in their communities. They expected that it would even go beyond their local communities and have a global impact.

ANOTHER MAN'S VISION
In the fall of 1993, Dr. Daniel Henderson and an elder from his church attended the North American Christian Leaders' Prayer Summit in Portland, Oregon. On the way home, their discussion turned to how the same kind of event could impact a local church. As the discussion progressed, Daniel became more and more convinced that this was what his comfortable, established church needed in order to be revitalized.

As Daniel sought advice about holding a Prayer Summit for his church, he was told not to try it. He was also told that the Prayer Summit could not be implemented in a local church. Additionally, he was told it would not work because the people of a local congregation would not sacrifice either the money or the time involved for three and one-half days away from home with the pastor to do nothing but

---

[1] God's face represents His character as opposed to His hand, which represents what He does.

pray. Daniel is fond of saying, "If you are not living on the edge, you are taking up too much space." True to living on the edge, he decided to go for it anyway.

Six months after accepting the position of Senior Pastor, Daniel Henderson announced that the church would hold a Prayer Summit. No one in the congregation knew what a Prayer Summit was, but around 100 people signed up anyway.

Chapter 2
How a Prayer Summit Changed My Life

When Pastor Daniel Henderson announced that our church[2] was going to hold a three-day Prayer Summit, I immediately signed up. Prayer was boring and hard for me, and any help I could get would be welcome. However, I did have a little trouble with the three-day part. After all, who could pray for three days? But then again, my list of prayer requests would take a considerable amount of time. I assumed that much of the time would be spent in lectures on how to pray, and God knew I needed that. Besides, many of my friends had signed up; judging from past conferences, we would have great fun together during the "free time."

I caught a ride with a friend to the Christian conference hotel, just outside of Chico, California, where the Prayer Summit was held. We arrived in time for dinner with the others who were registered for this new experience. I felt a high level of expectation and excitement – until the first session.

During the first session, Pastor Daniel explained that a Prayer Summit was simply a gathering of people who took seriously their responsibility of prayer in order to prepare for the outpouring of God's blessing. He stated that there would be times of prolonged praise and prayer and that we could expect personal revival through repentance and reconciliation. He also noted that there might be times of "spiritual warfare" as we were led to deal with areas of personal and/or corporate sin. That statement triggered a little uneasiness, but I ignored it.

---

[2] Arcade Church, Sacramento, California

Daniel went on to say that we would be seeking who God is, not what He could do. So the prayer lists and requests, which we might have brought with us, would not be addressed at this Prayer Summit. And there would not be teaching on prayer. Okay, now I had a larger sense of uneasiness. What in the world were we going to do if we wouldn't pray for these things or attend lectures on how to pray?

He then explained that the format would be prayer, singing, scripture reading, and personal response. He gave the guidelines, which included being sensitive to others, connecting with what was going on, listening, and observing times of silence. Daniel stated that a variety of expressions were encouraged. He explained further:

> Some will choose to sit, and some will kneel. Others may stand, walk, or lay prostrate. Some will sing and worship with eyes open. Others with worship with eyes closed. Some may pray lifting their hands, and some will not. Our focus is on God, not one another. Because we want this singular focus to be very intense, we encourage participants to use whatever 'forms' will best help them focus on the Lord.

He then said, "We have no agenda for these three days. We don't know what we are going to do. We will just follow the leading of the Holy Spirit."

Now I was feeling full-blown panic! I had no experience with the term "spiritual warfare" and so equated it with dark movies I had seen. As far as the varieties of expressions, this sounded like total chaos—everyone doing whatever they felt like. My extremely conservative, to some degree legalistic, background told me that this might not be biblical or pleasing to God. But the last statement about not having an agenda, not knowing what we were going to do – just "follow the Holy Spirit" – was more than I was prepared to accept. I had little to no understanding of the Holy Spirit as a person that I could hear from, communicate with, rely on, or follow. As a result this sounded like something in which I should not be involved.

I was enveloped with fear, panic, and stomach cramps. I was physically ill. I was trapped. I could not leave because I had come with someone else, and she was staying.

Thus began my personal experience with "spiritual warfare," although, at the time I might not have called it that. As I climbed into my bunk bed, in a room I shared with eight other women, the tears began to flow as I sought God's forgiveness for being there.

Some 10 years before, I had willingly entered into an occult experience from which God had delivered and forgiven me. I had promised Him that I never again would attend or participate in anything that was not totally of Him. I would never again have anything to do with the things of the kingdom of darkness. And now, here I was in a situation that did not sound like any prayer gathering I had ever attended. This was a situation I could not get out of, and it caused me to fear that my participation would not be pleasing to God and might cause me to break my promise to Him. I was distraught.

I did not get much sleep that night as I fought the battle. I could not get peace about my fears. Finally, I fully surrendered to Him stating:

> *Lord, I don't know what I am doing here. Only you know. If I am somewhere I should not be please, rescue me. Protect me from all harm and plans of the enemy. If you want me to leave, provide a way. I cast myself upon your mercy. Help me please!*

God did not rescue me or provide a way out. Not only did I attend all the sessions, but I also participated. During the days that followed, I experienced personal renewal and revival through the revelation of who God really is—His character—and that I truly could trust Him, no matter what.

This began a great change in my relationship with the Lord, a change from one of distance to one of intimacy. This change encompassed my truly surrendered heart and life. This new relationship proved to be critical to my survival during future trials and tribulations, abounding with circumstances in which I would have been defeated except that I had discovered an intimate, dependent oneness with Christ.

CHAPTER 3
STORIES OF PERSONAL TRANSFORMATION

Many of the people who have attended a Prayer Summit have a testimony of dramatic life-change. People attend for different reasons, but nearly everyone has a unique personal encounter with God.

Obedience
Jim, a skeptical but curious man, says:

> *I don't know why I attended my first Prayer Summit. I guess it was a step of obedience. God's searchlight on my heart was most significant. He revealed the wall of protection I had put up around my heart that locked out His blessing. As a result of attending this Prayer Summit, I have a renewed desire to seek God, to hear from Him, to express worship and to invest my time in prayer.*

Curious
Dixie Weyel, a longtime staff member at Arcade Church in Sacramento, CA, describes her decision to attend her first Prayer Summit:

> *I attended my first Prayer Summit because I trusted my pastor, Daniel Henderson, who had experienced one. I could see how it had impacted him. I wanted the nearness of God, and I was curious.*
>
> *What I experienced was fresh and new to me. I was very aware of the Lord's presence in the midst of our worship. My heart was crushed with the awareness of God's holiness and*

His worthiness to be adored and exalted. I have never wept like I did that weekend. The tears just came and came. He filled me so full of Himself and loved on me and caused me to hunger for more of Him. I knew I wanted to be clean in His presence because the awareness of Him shined light on the places I needed to confess. I gladly gave myself up, and He just continued to pour into me joy, peace, contentment, and eagerness to worship Him more.

I have not been the same since. My personal and corporate times of worship are much richer and sweeter. I now know the real meaning of a romance with Jesus. I don't just love Him; I am in love with Him. How amazing to know that my worship and praying are pleasing to Him. As I praise Him for who He is, all the concerns and questions of my life are laid to rest.

A Desire to Grow Closer to God
Rich, a civil engineer, gives his account:

I had some fear about what might happen at my first Prayer Summit, but my desire to draw closer to God motivated me to attend anyway. It radically transformed my devotional times. I learned how to worship God by seeking Him through His attributes. I learned to worship by quoting Scripture and singing. Through journaling, I see more clearly God's answers and direction. I truly sit at the feet of the Master—a God who loves even me.

A Gift from the Father
Don, a pastor, says:

When I attended my first Prayer Summit, the Lord took away my heart of stone and gave me a heart of flesh. I have rarely experienced anything like this. In that condensed period of time, the Lord did in me a powerful, wonderful and marvelous work that was permanent, life-transforming, and supernatural. The Prayer Summit was a gift from the Father.

Reluctant and Doubtful
Sandi Selland, a young mother, shares:

When my husband told me we were going to pray for tshree days at a Prayer Summit, I thought he had tipped his rocker back a wee bit too far. With all the depressing news of job losses and common physical ailments, I could barely sit through an hour of prayer, let alone three days' worth. Prayer meetings, in my experience, consisted of 55 minutes of grumbling and five minutes of praying. They were boring and ineffective; worse, they left me feeling depressed rather than uplifted. In short, I would rather pray alone than with a group of complainers. In my mind I thought, fine, we'll go and waste an entire weekend, and money, too. It'll be awful, full of old people griping about their corns and ingrown toe nails.

The first session began with a lot of instruction, and I realized this wasn't going to be the typical prayer meeting. Then we began to pray—or rather, praise the Lord. At first, people seemed to be uneasy with praying out loud, and there were a lot of pauses. Eventually the praises of God's people began to flow and mix with Scripture reading and song. A theme emerged, and we all began to head in the same direction. When the subject changed direction, so did God's people. It was beautiful. The most surprising and wonderful part was the felt presence of God. I could actually feel God's presence in that room with us, and I drank Him in as if I were parched soil absorbing the rain. I was completely caught up in the Spirit and enjoying every minute. When the facilitator said, 'as we conclude this evening . . .' I could hardly believe it. What I thought had taken ten minutes had actually gone over two hours, and still I wanted to keep going! I was refreshed and excited, and I couldn't wait for the next day's prayer session.

Each day got better and deeper. Then the final session on the last day erupted with outright joy. Our burdens had been lifted, our sins confessed, our guilt removed, our bonds broken—someone even got saved. We experienced God and His pleasure in us, in a very unique way, simply by praying together honestly and without judgment. Most amazing of all was I, the most reluctant attendee, was now loath to leave.

As you read these testimonies, you can't help but notice that each life was changed in some way. They all experienced personal renewal and revival. Their affections toward God were changed with a desire for more of God. They also became contagious and infected others with their passion for prayer, led by the Spirit, and based in worship.

These testimonies, and many more like them, express the heart of a local church Prayer Summit that "infects the affections."

CHAPTER 4
WHAT IS A LOCAL CHURCH PRAYER SUMMIT?

One pastor says that a Local Church Prayer Summit truly is a place where *"infection of the affections"* takes place. It's a place where people's attention and affection for God, worship, and prayer rise. The pastor considers it the fastest, most efficient and most effective way to develop a prayer culture in a church. It is training ground for a church to become a House of Prayer.

A Local Church Prayer Summit is a group of individuals from the same church congregation, led by their pastor, who commit to spending several days together seeking God's agenda and will for their lives, families, church, and community. It is a time and place where individuals of a local church body are prepared, through corporate worship and prayer, to expect an outpouring of God's blessing in a new profound way. It is a time and place:

- Where renewal in one's relationship with God commonly occurs.
- That promotes long-term unity among believers.
- For both a personal and a group encounter with God, where the participants experience the glory of Christ within and among them.
- Of prolonged praise and prayer during which individuals from the same church or group discover and express their oneness in Christ.
- And environment where personal revival is nurtured and commonly occurs.
- Of personal healing, forgiveness, and deliverance.
- For repentance and reconciliation.

- For spiritual warfare as Christians are led to deal with areas of personal and corporate sin.
- Where the church begins to become newly dependent on God.
- Where transparency between a pastor and his congregation allows for bonding, loyalty, and unity to take place.

We could describe the Local Church Prayer Summit as a modern-day form of the Old Testament Solemn (sacred) Assembly. When a Solemn Assembly was called, the people gathered together to honor God and to meet with Him. It was a time of restraint from work and other distractions, a time to confess sins and cry out to the Lord in repentance, and a time to pray for the His mercy. In his commentary on Joel, Warren Wiersbe states:

> *It's easy to participate in a religious ceremony, tear your garments, and lament, but quite some-thing else to humbly confess your sins and bring to God repentance. The one thing that encourages us to repent and return to the Lord is the character of God. Knowing that He is indeed gracious and compassionate, slow to anger and abounding in love ought to motivate us to seek His face.*[3]

Perhaps you are the pastor; you may have attended a Pastor's Prayer Summit and are not sure how to translate that experience into your local church body. Maybe you are the Prayer Coordinator at your church. Or, maybe you are one of the congregations who would like to have a Prayer Summit at your local church. In any case, the foremost questions on your mind may be:

- What is the purpose and goal of a Local Church Prayer Summit?
- What are the benefits for the church and community?
- What is involved in planning and preparation?
- Where and how do I start?
- How does one lead a Local Church Prayer Summit?
- What are the keys to success?
- Are there resources available to help one plan a Local Church Prayer Summit?

---

[3] Warren W. Wiersbe, *The Bible Exposition Commentary: Old Testament*, Joel 1:14, 2:15

In addition to Local Church Prayer Summits, there are Pastor's Prayer Summits, women's or men's summits, and summits for married couples. There can be Prayer Summits for children or youth, or for entire families. Each of these will have a different impact on the local church as a whole, resulting in varying benefits to the body. However, basic planning and preparation are important for all Prayer Summits, regardless of the group composition. They all have a single purpose and focus—to seek the presence of God through spirit-led, worship-based prayer,[4] not for what He might do, but just because He is worthy to be worshiped and sought after. He is God!

When the focus is on God, the lasting impact will instill a desire for people to experience the presence of God through worship and the leading of the Spirit in every prayer gathering at their church. Meetings with God will be so meaningful and powerful that the people will long for more of Him. A change of directional focus, from horizontal to vertical, happens within the entire church. It results in changed lives that have become infected with new love for God, and His presence, to such a degree that people are contagious and infect others, and every ministry with whom they come in contact. There will be an *"infection of the affections."*

For our purpose, we are going to focus on a Prayer Summit for married and single adults[5], sponsored by a local church. We will refer to this hereafter as the "Local Church Prayer Summit" (LCPS).

Sometimes there is a tendency to hold the first church Prayer Summit for either all men or all women. I would advise you not to do that. There are great advantages to a mixed group, which has a greater impact when the summit is over and the people return to their ministries.

As you read the following pages, you will not only find practical answers to your questions, but the anticipation and excitement of what God will do at your Local Church Prayer Summit will increase immeasurably.

---

[4] For a description of "Worship-Based" prayer, see Appendix A
[5] "Adults" means over the age of 18.

CHAPTER 5
BENEFITS OF THE LOCAL CHURCH PRAYER SUMMIT FOR THE PARTICIPANT

I was called out of the first session of our Prayer Summit to take a phone call from someone who had gotten lost trying to find the location of the summit.

In the warmth of the excitement and anticipation of what God would do at this particular Prayer Summit, I was unprepared for the anger, abruptness, and criticism from the man on the other end of the phone. He had missed the turnoff to the retreat grounds twice and was not only frustrated, but also very angry. It was dark, and he felt that if we had prepared better directions, he would not be lost. I listened to him rage about our incompetence and bad directions. When he finally drew a breath, I gave him directions to the turnoff.

I hung up and called together several people and we prayed fervently for this man. We asked God to take away his anger and change his attitude. We asked God to meet him at his point of need during this summit.

When he arrived, we could not miss the scowl on his very angry red face. We tried to make him feel welcome, but it appeared that he didn't really want to be there. Early on during the meetings he was aloof, standing and pacing about the perimeter of the group.

We learned that he was the pastor of a church that was experiencing intense conflict and struggles, and because he was the pastor, all of the increasing unrest and criticism fell upon him. He stated:

> *I had exhausted the strategy of finding the one 'fix' that would solve my church's problems and I was frustrated over all the details of ministry. No matter what I tried it was not enough. I had no expectation that I would find the answers, or even peace, at this Prayer Summit. I was ready to turn around and go home.*

However, we knew that this man had not escaped God's notice and that he was not at this summit by accident. God had arranged a divine appointment with him. God had a plan and a purpose to begin healing this man's shattered life through His people. During a time of worship-based prayer, scripture reading, and singing, God broke through the shield the pastor had put up around himself. Psalm 51:17 says, "I learned God-worship when my pride was shattered. Heart-shattered lives ready for love don't for a moment escape God's notice."[6] This man experienced "God-worship." He said:

> *I was struck by the 100 or so people who had gathered to pray. I was also amazed at the sense of God's presence and the beauty of worship as the people corporately lifted their voices to God in psalms, hymns, and praise songs. This was not a typical request-based prayer meeting; rather, it was a symphony of praise and prayer to God for all that He is and what He has done. I felt like I was in a dream as I experienced the love and unity that accompanied the Prayer Summit.*
>
> *It seemed that my inner turmoil would not stop even as I tried to enter into the worship. But as the emphasis turned to self-examination and confession, I had my encounter with God, and I surrendered afresh to the Holy Spirit. I was able to release all my agendas, my personal resentment, and anger as I put all I valued on the altar before Jesus. I was truly renewed by the grace of God, and a sense of freedom and restoration came over me. The rest of the summit was pure joy as the Lord ministered to my spirit.*

During one of the men's small group meetings, brothers gathered around him as he shared his disappointment, rejection, pain, and hurt. They encouraged him, prayed for him, and showed him the

---

[6] Eugene H. Peterson, The Message Bible

love of God. Their support did not stop at the summit; rather they continued to pray for him on a regular basis. Many supported and encouraged him for several years as he continued to experience God's healing.

Discovering the Power of Worship-Based Prayer

Minister and author, E. M. Bounds said:

> God puts a great price on humility . . . That which brings the praying soul near to God is humility of heart. That which gives wings to prayer is lowliness of mind. It gives access to God when other qualities fail.[7]

Worship-based prayer is the foundation of a Prayer Summit, and all else flows from that position of humility. There can be no harbored pride, personal agenda, or church agenda if the desire is to truly enter into the glorious presence of the most Holy God.

We must passionately desire to relate intimately to Him on His terms. Worship and praise is the language of spiritual lovers, which brings about the discovery of the pleasure and joy of God's presence. One cannot enter the presence of God through worship without experiencing both short-term and long-term benefits. After all, God is the one who said, "Seek my face."[8]

In His presence, we soon realize that prayer is not a monologue of our needs and wants, but a yearning for a real relationship. The pleasure of just being in God's presence with like-minded people, as experienced at a Prayer Summit, transcends time; the intimidation of spending several days praying no longer exists. What actually happens is that, even after several hours in the glory of God's presence, no one wants to leave or wants the worship to end. The time together seems much too short.

In many, if not most, churches the united church prayer meeting has been eliminated. Thus, the priority of praying as a body together has diminished. At a Prayer Summit, many experience the dynamics of personal growth for the first time through united prayer.

---

[7] E. M. Bounds, *The Essentials of Prayer (Baker, 1987)*, p. 21
[8] See Psalm 27:8, as well as 2 Chronicles 2:7 and Hosea 5:15 NKJV

Beyond Individualism

We in the Western world live in a "high-tech" environment and society that encourages independence, individualism, and isolation. Through the internet, e-mail, blogs, Twitter, Facebook, etc., we communicate without face-to-face interaction. We have relegated our communication to little more than the "virtual–reality" of the make-believe world. And the danger exists that this short-circuited, abbreviated, multitasked pattern will carry over into our communication with God.

When we ask for prayer and when we are asked to pray for others, if we embrace these modern tools and the exclusion of face-to-face interaction, our communication and prayer all too often take on impersonal qualities, lacking any real emotional involvement or investment. Without personal contact, we forfeit both the tone of someone's voice and the comfort of hearing their voice fervently praying for us. Facial expressions, hugs when we are hurting, the comfort of someone weeping with us, and the touch of a human hand on our shoulder are missing. We also discard the promise of Jesus when He said, "I say to you, that if two of you agree on earth concerning anything that they ask, it will be done for them by My Father in Heaven. For where two or three are *gathered together* in My name, I am there in the midst of them"[9] (emphasis added).

There is no question that these tools have a place in our interaction with each other. However, when they become the primary way we pray for others and ask others to pray for us, we are robbed of the blessings God intended for us as we gather together, face-to-face. As a result, we tend to live lives independent of each other and God.

Mutual Impact

The structure of the Prayer Summit is such that we are brought to the stark realization of our need for and dependence on God and others. We are astounded at the impact of someone's tears shed because of our pain. We are comforted when we hear someone's voice as they pray for us. Our faith grows and we have hope when we hear God's Word proclaimed. We are encouraged when we hear the testimony of someone who has faced the same trials we have, and we realize they have survived and become stronger. We are often amazed and delighted at how God uses others to minister to us, and vice versa.

---

[9] Matthew 18:19,20 NKJV

At a Prayer Summit, as we seek God together and pray for one another for healing,[10] we see the words of Jesus fulfilled when He says, "He has sent Me to heal the broken-hearted, to preach deliverance to the captives, and to set free those who are oppressed."[11]

Broken-hearted
Anna, a pastor's wife, says:

> *I came to the Prayer Summit broken-hearted, wounded, and discouraged. I was physically and emotionally ill from the battle. From the very beginning of the summit, God pursued me to come close to Him. I wasn't even sure I could. I was tired and angry at Him and some of His people in my church. God is faithful, and He led me to the river of healing, forgiveness, and reconciliation. He pursued me as Jehovah Rapha[12] and Jehovah Shalom [13]and began healing my broken heart.*

One man, estranged from both God and people, states:

> *In my brokenness I wanted to get back to God—to put Him as number one in my life. I was brought face-to-face with the sadness that I had for having wandered from Him for so many years. My life was impacted to just trust God and return to fellowship at my church.*

Oppressed
Erika, a discouraged young woman, reports:

> *I was able to bring all my burdens to the foot of the cross, and Jesus set me free from my unresolved past and hurt. He gave me a fresh start in my life and confirmed that He will be my strength.*

Carol, a woman full of anxiety, says:

> *God spoke to me through His Word and other sources about an area of my life that I had taken lightly: worry and anxiety. It is sin, and I cannot allow it to dwell in me if I want fellowship with God. I needed others to pray for me to have victory.*

---

[10] James 5:16 NKJV
[11] Luke 4:18 NKJV
[12] Jehovah Rapha-The LORD who heals, Exodus 15:25-27
[13] Jehovah Shalom-The LORD is peace, Numbers 6:22-27

Delivered
A woman, broken and defeated, testifies:

> *I agreed to go to the Prayer Summit at the urging of my sister. However, my plans were to commit suicide the following Tuesday, on my birthday. I had been told that because of my many problems and depression, I could not possibly be a Christian. My abusive family never wanted me, and now I felt that God didn't want me, either. There was no reason to live.*
>
> *At one of the small groups, I knelt before the symbolic chair where Jesus was sitting and began to pour out my heart. I was surrounded by women who began to pray and plead with God for me. I immediately felt love, relief, and peace. I knew that there had been a significant change in me. I lost all desire to take my life. I wanted to live!*
>
> *I now know that God does want me. I now wake up every morning happy, at peace, and with a reason to live–all because I attended a Prayer Summit and met God face-to-face.*

A Powerful Shared Experience

The essence of these testimonies is repeated over and over by people who have attended a Local Church Prayer Summit.

As a group of people from the same church comes together for an extended period of time to seek God in prayer, their hearts soften toward each other, and a permanent bond takes place. Understanding, compassion, and forgiveness flow freely, creating the love for one another that Jesus commanded.[14] When individual members of a congregation experience the personal presence and touch of Christ; the entire body benefits from the overflow and the blessing of grace.

After several different LCPSs, the summit coordinators asked, "How did this Prayer Summit impact you?" The attendees gave the following responses:

- The Lord showed me the importance of dedicated obedience, submitting to Him daily, moment by moment.
- I learned to listen to God. He taught me to be still.

---

[14] John 13:34, John 15:12, John 15:17

- I learned to worship by seeking His face instead of always asking.
- I was able to be transparent and honest with Him.
- He taught me to worship and share my burden with others.
- I learned that silence can be of the Spirit.
- I was able to forgive those who caused me great pain.
- God took away the anxiety of being exposed to Him and others.
- I learned how to incorporate Scripture into my personal worship by praying it back to God.
- I enjoyed an intimacy with God that I did not know existed or was possible.
- I experienced a love for my pastor that I did not have before. I am committed to praying for him daily.
- I received spiritual renewal and a deep sense of peace.
- I learned the value and importance of focusing entirely upon God rather than being distracted by always trying to please people.
- Prayer with others is becoming a priority for me.
- God did a great work in my life by breaking chains and building relationships.
- Most significant was listening to and soaking in all the scripture.
- I learned how to praise through the Spirit and His people.
- I have a new perspective and appreciation for the power of the Word of God, worship, and prayer to heal brokenness and to change lives in all areas: heart, spirit, mind, body, and soul.

These testimonies give us a glimpse of God's touch at a LCPS; however, people often say, "You cannot begin to describe God's presence at a Prayer Summit; you have to experience it."

Our Western thinking places knowledge as the intellectual expression of reality and the affirmation of perceived truth. By contrast, in Hebrew and Greek, the word "know," in addition to cognitive knowing, has a purely experiential side. To know God is to have an intimate experiential knowledge of Him. [15]

Noted author, Brennan Manning puts it this way, "It is simply not possible to receive the revelation of God in the transcendent/

---

[15] Vines Expository Dictionary of Biblical Words (OT & NT)

immanent Christ without experience. Experience is an essential part of knowing Jesus and of the whole concept of revelation."[16]

When we experience the dynamics of a LCPS, the old concept of corporate prayer consisting of long and boring prayer lists, much discussion of requests, pious recitations intended as prayer, and time dragging on forever, is challenged. Because people who attend a LCPS have experienced the presence and touch of God through a united prayer gathering, they often return to their church with a burning desire to continue the experience and to replicate the Prayer Summit pattern of corporate prayer in their church. They have been *infected with new affection* for God.

---

[16] Brennan Manning, *Ruthless Trust*, (Harper One, 2000), pg. 87, 88

CHAPTER 6
BENEFITS OF THE LOCAL CHURCH PRAYER SUMMIT FOR THE PASTOR

There is no question that the return of a congregation's burning desire for corporate prayer is a blessing and benefit for the pastor, the church body, and the community. For we know that unity and God's power are abundantly experienced through united prayer. However, if the people of the church return to the same pattern of prayer meeting they had experienced before, the burning desire will quickly die out and there will be a return to sparsely-attended, corporate prayer meetings or no corporate prayer meetings at all.

Andrew Murray stated:

> *Prayer is the pulse of life; by it the doctor can tell what the condition of the heart is. The sin of prayerlessness is a proof, for the ordinary Christian, or minister, that the life of God, in the soul, is in deadly sickness and weakness.*[17]

To go along with that, I say, "Our prayerlessness is our declaration of independence from God."

The same could be said about a church body that has neglected or abandoned corporate prayer. Indeed the prayerless church is in danger of Jesus' description, and judgment of the Laodicean Church in the book of Revelation.[18] He said that because they were only lukewarm, neither cold nor hot, He would vomit them out of His mouth. It is interesting that He described them as wretched, miserable,

---
[17] Andrew Murray, *The Prayer Life,* (Whitaker House 1987), p.15
[18] Revelation 3:14-22

poor, blind and naked—and they did not know it. Likewise, today, a prayerless church fits that description, and does not know it.

A church that neglects corporate prayer sends the message that they are rich, have become wealthy and have a need of nothing. In their declaration of independence from God, their works are in their own strength, not in the power of God, and therefore are worthless in God's sight.

Pastor Mark Vroegop, Senior Pastor of College Park Church in Indianapolis, Indiana, describes the typical prayer meeting and the difference a Prayer Summit made in the way he now leads his church in prayer. He said:

> *In my role as a pastor, I often over controlled when I gave specific direction as to what we should pray and how we should pray. Tragically, this usually meant another devotional, a long list of prayer requests, and very little allowance for the direction of the Holy Spirit. There was very little actual worship or prayer. Although worship was a stated commitment in our prayer times, it wasn't practiced as a priority. Worship was the prelude to the "real" praying, which were requests. The people were not satisfied, and so they weren't coming back. Then, we over-spiritualized by making excuses for the lack of attendance by trying to convince ourselves, and others, that the problem was with the people's spiritual maturity and worldly involvements, not the way the prayer meeting was conducted.*

Vroegop then describes the power of a Prayer Summit:

> *After attending a Prayer Summit and bringing worship-based prayer into our prayer meetings, worship became the defining mark. Suddenly people experienced God and left the meetings more in love with Him. I heard people say, "So, we're doing this again, right?" When we engage the three Prayer Summit elements—the Spirit leading, the direct use of Scripture in forming our prayers, and spontaneous singing—worship just happens. All else is built and flows from that worship. Prayer becomes the response to who God is, instead of requests of what I need Him to do. The difference was a shift in who was really leading. It was a small shift, but at*

> *the same time it was a major shift, and it affected every prayer meeting I led. It changed the directional focus from horizontal to vertical. Adding that dimension was both appealing and beautiful. Frankly, this gave the prayer meeting a lot of life. The Spirit was given the opportunity to lead our people instead of me leading. I didn't understand this difference until I experienced free flowing Spirit-fed prayer at a Prayer Summit.*

Lindsay Taylor, pastor of Rothesay Baptist Church in Quispamsis, New Brunswick, testifies:

> *I came to the place of absolute frustration with the traditional prayer meeting and the lack of attendance. As the pastor, I cancelled our prayer service. I personally had enjoyed many incredible times of prayer that included group settings, Scripture reading, and songs being sung. After several months, the Spirit prompted me to lead worship and prayer, and that began a journey for me.*
>
> *I began to lead prayer with worship instead of simply allowing repeated, request-based prayer. I began to read and study more in the Bible, and historical sources, to learn how in the past, in response to prayer, God had worked mightily and miraculously through His people, and the early Christian church. I developed the absolute conviction that He could do the same, again, today. The response from the church was fantastic.*

The beauty and transparency of corporate, Spirit-fed prayer during the LCPS encourages honesty before God and has been proven to stimulate repentance. Often, mountains of sins have built up in a congregation until they seem insurmountable, sins that paralyze a church body into passivity, such as lukewarm-ness and other sins that make a church body comfortable with prayerlessness.

If there is to be a lasting impact for change in the local church, the pastor must be the one to lead and sustain the movement of Spirit-led, worship-based, corporate prayer in his congregation. A worship-based Prayer Summit sets the stage for the pastor and his congregation to experience the difference between man-led and Spirit-led prayer. By the Holy Spirit's leading, the pastor is enabled to lead his congregation into the presence of God, where they become excited and are satisfied with His goodness, who He is rather than staying self-focused on what they want God to do.

Vroegop and Taylor were asked why they thought a Prayer Summit, modeling worship-based prayer, was an important priority in bringing their people together in prayer. Their answers exhibit several benefits for both the pastor and the congregation.

Vroegop said:

> *As a pastor, I must be involved with my people by praying with them. So I think, for a Senior Pastor, something like a Prayer Summit is critical and important because the calling, as pastors, is to the word and prayer. That's the essence of a pastor's calling. In order to be able to help the people both learn to pray, and to bring prayer into church ministry, it can't be just a program, and it can't be just teaching.*
>
> *The people know that they are supposed to pray. I know I'm supposed to pray. We know how to pray. The problem is not that we don't know the value of prayer. It's a desire problem. Two or three days at a Prayer Summit helps the desire problem. The result of a Prayer Summit is that the attention and affection rise. The summit creates a reorientation of the heart, and once people taste it, they won't be the same. The result is that they will change how they minister in the areas where they are already serving.*

Regarding the importance of a Prayer Summit in bringing a congregation together in prayer, Taylor replied:

> *I absolutely think that corporate prayer, practiced regularly and led by the pastor of the church, is important. It is critical that the people see the Senior Pastor committed to the ministry and discipline of prayer. If we, pastors, truly believe that prayer is the hard work of ministry, then we need to model that conviction. People seem to learn more from our example than our preaching. The benefits of communion with God in a corporate setting are inexhaustible. To see God's people set on fire, by Christ, helps bring about a sense of dependence upon God as well as renewal, revival, and unity, all benefits of the Prayer Summit experience.*

Dennis Fuqua is the Executive Director of International Renewal Ministries, headquartered in Portland, Oregon. This ministry carries out the vision of the late Dr. Joseph Aldrich by sponsoring dozens of Prayer Summits all around the world. Fuqua relates:

> *When I was in Bible college, a friend told me how he had been observing what took place in the typical Sunday morning church service. He listed off several items and said, "Then he does the pastoral prayer, which lasts between two minutes and two minutes, seventeen seconds." I laughed, and he told me that he had actually timed it. From time to time, I checked his timing in different churches, and he was pretty accurate.*

Fuqua continues:

> *It seems that most of the training in prayer that a believer receives from the typical church comes from hearing the pastoral prayer on Sunday morning, hearing other prayers from the pulpit, or participating in small groups when asked, "What are your prayer requests?" When these are the only instructions or examples one receives, it communicates that praying is done only by the professional or someone who is experienced. It also communicates that prayer is primarily about having needs and desires met. Prayer is sometimes mentioned in the sermon, but rarely is there an opportunity for the attendee to engage in prayer in a personal, meaningful way.*

Speaking on the impact of a summit, Fuqua concludes:

> *The Prayer Summit is an opportunity for people to get a new perspective on what prayer is all about. It allows people to develop deeper relationships with the people around them as well as God. It invites people to listen and speak to the Lord while others listen in and agree. This kind of worship-based, corporate prayer requires that the pastor approaches prayer differently than he may have had in the past. Instead of the leader "leading in prayer" and the people listening and nodding, the leader assists as they pray. The primary difference for us pastors comes when we move from seeing ourselves as the "leader" to seeing ourselves as a "facilitator."*

Pastors Experiencing Freedom

A major benefit for the pastor, as a result of hosting and leading a LCPS occurs on a personal level. Before experiencing a Prayer Summit, many pastors feel insecure and fear criticism, rejection and resistance to their leadership. As a result, they maintain aloofness from the people of their congregation as a protective measure. In the Prayer Summit setting, which encourages transparency and unconditional acceptance by everyone; these fears tend to dissipate, with positive results for the pastor.

The Prayer Summit setting allows a pastor to know his people in a way that is not possible in the church setting. In part, this is due to time constraints, but more important is the opportunity for the pastor to hear his people worship God, praise Him, and pray from a position of humility and submission that is often missing in church meetings where time is limited. The nature of extended time during a Prayer Summit tends to be conducive to more complete, sincere, and honest communication with God and each other.

As the pastor, along with the congregation, submits to the leading of the Holy Spirit, he becomes one of the participants, rather than merely the leader. As a result, he enters into worship freely and his prayers change tone, reflecting his heart.

In 1996, Pastor Don Carson of Grass Valley, California, attended his first LCPS held by Arcade Church. He writes of that experience, "There were no agendas, no preaching, and no tight schedules. The whole time was spent seeking the face of God, worshiping, praying, and reading Scripture." Carson further describes the experience:

> *As the Holy Spirit led us, we confessed sin and were encouraged and supported by each other in love and acceptance. The Lord met with us in unusual and special ways. It was a time of revival and renewal. The Lord took away my heart of stone and gave me a heart of flesh. The Lord did, in a condensed period of time, a powerful, wonderful, supernatural, life-transforming work. Deep commitments were made. Significant spiritual and emotional issues were dealt with. Trust, safety, and intimacy were developed. Hard hearts were broken, sin patterns were confessed, and accountability was earnestly sought. Arrogance and pride were dealt with.*

In expressing the impact of a Summit, Don Carson states:

> The atmosphere was totally safe where people could cry out to God with each other, and His love, grace, and forgiveness would sweep over them. Dynamic love for one another was the immediate result. The Lord met me at that Prayer Summit, and I will never be the same.

Experiencing Genuine Worship

Observing the pastor worship in this way has a profound impact on the people. As they see and experience the sincerity and transparency of their pastor's heart, they are not only willing but also eager to follow his leading. A bonding and knitting of hearts take place. New understanding, respect, tolerance, and love emerge, demonstrated by a lessening of aloofness on the part of the pastor. Acceptance, support and a willingness to follow the pastor's leading are reactions of the people. Lifelong friendships and loyalty begin. Commitments to pray regularly for the pastor are commonly made.

As the pastor allows himself to be vulnerable, a realization dawns on the people that he is not different in the eyes of God. He just has a different calling, which results in different responsibilities. The tendencies to consider him some kind of "super-spiritual" person, put him on a pedestal, or hold him to unrealistic standards, disappear.

While attending a Prayer Summit, the pastor will find that he is in a place where he can be ministered to and supported without fear of judgment by the people. He, too, will experience a changed heart. And when he returns to ministry in his church, the people will sense the change in his heart. They will know that he is not the same as before the summit, and they will want to follow his leading. He will have had his *"affections infected"* and be ready to infect the congregation.

PART II

Planning the Summit

Chapter 7
The Keys to a Successful Local Church Prayer Summit

There was a man who threw a great dinner party and invited many. When it was time for dinner, he sent out his servant to the invited guests saying, "Come on in. The food's on the table."

Then they all began make excuses, one after another. The first said, "I bought a piece of property and need to look it over. Send my regrets."

Another said, "I just bought five teams of oxen, and I really need to check them out. Send my regrets."

And yet another said, "I just got married and need to get home to my wife."

The servant went back and told the master what had happened.[19]

Because no one wants to plan an event that people do not attend, the question we have is this, "What are the keys to success for a Local Church Prayer Summit?"

At a LCPS, we want to experience and advance the Kingdom of Heaven. We want to enter into the very presence of God Almighty in His throne room. That would be success! So what are the keys that unlock God's presence, the throne room, at a Prayer Summit?

---

[19] Eugene H. Peterson, *The Message*, Luke 14: 16-21a

Prayer that Advances Prayer

There is only one key, and that is prayer. The very purpose of a Prayer Summit is prayer. The intent and goal is not to talk about prayer, but to pray. Not to talk about God, but to meet and talk with Him. Not to seek man's agenda, but to seek God's agenda, both individually and corporately. And that key, prayer, should be used and practiced, from a pastor's first thoughts and desires to host a LCPS through all the planning and preparation.

Prayer as the key may seem like an obvious statement. However, if not protected, prayer in preparation and planning will be neglected either in practice or the time allowed for prayer.

Prayer should begin with the pastor as he prays about hosting a LCPS, and then as he goes about the selection and appointment of the Summit Coordinator. Prayer for the summit in general should be stressed and modeled by both the pastor and the Summit Coordinator in every meeting and decision as they plan for the summit.

The entire congregation should be encouraged to pray for the summit through the pastor's example and leading. The pastor should request that the congregation prays for those responsible for planning the summit as well as those who will attend. Congregational prayer should begin as soon as it is decided to host a LCPS, and it should continue through the finish of the summit.

Prayer should be an intentional, scheduled agenda item for every meeting in preparation for the LCPS. A good guideline is dedicating one-third of the meeting time to prayer. For example, in a two-hour meeting, 40 minutes should be set aside for prayer. For example, this would be divided into 30 minutes at the beginning of the meeting (20 minutes to worship and 10 minutes for intercession and requests) and 10 minutes at the close for praise and thanksgiving.

If this seems intimidating, remember that the goal is prayer, talking to God and seeking His agenda, His plans, and what He wants, even in—particularly in—the planning stage. If the thought arises that you may not have enough time to attend to all the necessary business, reject it. God has a way of redeeming the time, and there is always enough time when He is given first place.

As all the people involved in the planning process become comfortable with extended time in prayer, you will find that they will desire more time to pray and that some will stay after the meeting is adjourned, praying together just to bask in the presence of God.

As a result of giving God a prominent place, through prayer, in the planning of the summit, God will bless the Planning Committee members with joy, delight, excitement, and enthusiasm. All of these will be evident to others with whom they come in contact, and their attitude will spread and have an impact on people's desire to attend the LCPS.

Chapter 8
Key People

Although prayer is the only key to a successful Local Church Prayer Summit, certainly key people are required to carry out the details involved in planning and preparing for the summit.

SENIOR PASTOR

The first key person is the Senior Pastor of the church hosting the LCPS. Ideally, he will be the one to initiate the Prayer Summit, although this does not need to be the case. At any rate, the planning and preparation for a LCPS should start with the Senior Pastor, even if the initial idea or request does not come from him.

The pastor's responsibility will primarily be in encouraging attendance at the summit, teaching his congregation about the importance of and need for corporate prayer, teaching and preparing Prayer Facilitators, assisting the Summit Coordinator in making major decisions during the planning process, and leading at the summit itself.

He should be the one to seek and appoint a coordinator for the Prayer Summit. He should meet regularly with this person. He should convey clearly his vision for the LCPS and be available for suggestions and problem-solving. He should be involved in the initial formation of policies and procedures.

The degree of the pastor's approval of, support for, promotion of, and enthusiasm for the LCPS will have a profound effect on the congregation's acceptance of and participation in the LCPS. His attitude will also determine the long-term benefits that his church will enjoy, not the least of which is a spirit of unity and strong support of him.

The pastor should have a clear vision in mind for the LCPS and should be able to articulate it. The vision will only come as he spends extended time in prayer, seeking God's vision for the LCPS.

Dennis Fuqua of International Renewal Ministries says, "A Prayer Summit must be driven by the pastor's vision. Stating the vision in many different ways is necessary to relay that his heart is full [of anticipation], regarding what God will do for His people through the summit."

The personal preparation of the pastor is vital in preparing for a summit. He must continue to call out to God in his personal times of prayer, not simply for other people who will attend, but for his own heart, as well. The pastor should pray that God would show him more of Himself and help him to fall more deeply in love with God.

If not already trained, the pastor will need to teach and train Prayer Facilitators.[20] If he is not comfortable doing this himself, he can make arrangements for someone else to do so.[21] The pastor should provide opportunities for the facilitators to practice in small prayer groups for several weeks before the actual summit.

PRAYER SUMMIT COORDINATOR

Next to the pastor, the key person is the Prayer Summit Coordinator. This person will act as liaison among the pastor, the Summit Committee, the site staff, and others as necessary.

The Prayer Summit Coordinator should be appointed by the Senior Pastor and should be someone the pastor knows well, trusts, and in whom he has confidence. He/she will be responsible to keep the pastor up to date on the Summit Committee activities and meet with the Senior Pastor regularly during the planning process.

---

[20] See Appendix C for a sample training outline.
[21] Contact Strategic Renewal for referrals. See Resource section for contact information.

Qualities of Prayer Summit Coordinator:

- Should be able to delegate the planning and preparation so the pastor does not need to be directly involved in the process.
- Should include the pastor on important decisions that need to be made.
- Should already be involved in prayer and the Word; someone who is passionate about prayer.
- Should be humble, a person of integrity and have a good reputation.
- Should be spiritually mature with an ability to influence others to do what they think they don't want to do.
- Should be sympathetic and friendly, have an established network of friends, and inspire confidence.
- Should demonstrate spiritual gifts of organization, leadership, hospitality, teaching, and faith.
- Should exhibit the ability to hear and discern God's will and direction.
- Should be a good communicator who thinks independently and is capable of making clear decisions.
- Should be able to handle criticism and still act as peacemaker.
- Should be reasonably optimistic and not become discouraged or defeated by setbacks.
- Should be able to prioritize and manage details and not feel overwhelmed by them.
- Should demonstrate the ability to recognize the gifts of others and be able and willing to confidently delegate the needed responsibilities.
- Should not be dictatorial or domineering, rather demonstrate with confidence the authority to do the job, or task assigned, without meddling.

SUMMIT COMMITTEE

The Summit Coordinator will appoint the Summit Committee and assign job duties to the committee members. Each member of the Summit Committee is key to success in planning for a LCPS.

The Summit Committee should reflect the targeted make-up of the summit—a combination of men and women, married and single. Some responsibilities should be assigned to married couples and some to single people. Choose both people who are new to the church as well as those who are established. Choose people who represent the age range of the church adult membership. Look for people exhibiting spiritual gifts needed according to the committee Positions listed in Chapter Ten.

Committee members should have a desire to grow in their prayer lives. They should be growing in spiritual maturity. They should have a good reputation and a servant's heart. Look for people who have exhibited the quality of being a team player.

PRAYER FACILITATORS

At the LCPS, the Prayer Facilitators are responsible for the spiritual oversight and direction of the entire summit. They are the ones who usher the group into the presence of God. Therefore, the appointment of facilitators, for both large and small group meetings, is extremely important to the function of the summit.

At a LCPS, everyone meets together in a large group for a major portion of the Prayer Summit. But there is also time allowed for meeting together in gender-specific, small groups for more intimate sharing.

At a LCPS, there is one primary prayer leader, called the Primary Point, who leads the large combined group and sets the tone and pace for the entire summit. Ideally, this is the Senior Pastor. He will appoint assistants to help him, usually two to four people, and he will also select the point people and assistants for the small groups. The number of these will vary according to the number and gender make-up of those who are registered to attend the summit. For example, for a registration of 120 people (70 women and 50 men), five small groups would be needed: three for women and two for men. This would allow the number in each group to be under 30. It is desirable to keep each group at no more than 30, for intimacy and to allow time for everyone who wishes to share. A group between 25 and 30 is most desirable. Too small a group is also a hindrance to sharing.

Using this registration makeup, the total Prayer Facilitator team would be as follows:

For the large group:
- One Primary Point (usually the Senior Pastor)
- Two to four assistants (both men and women) to assist the Primary Point. These assistants can be, but don't need to, the ones who are appointed to facilitate the small groups.

For the small groups:

- The Senior Pastor should appoint one point and two assistants for each of the five small groups. Five points (two men and three women) and ten small group assistants will be needed (six women and four men).

Using this example, the Senior Pastor would need to appoint and train a total of 18 to 20 people to be Prayer Facilitators. This number will need to be adjusted according to the number of participants registered. Because the small groups are gender specific, they are the biggest factor that will affect the make-up and number of facilitators that are needed.

Qualities of a Prayer Facilitator

A Prayer Facilitator should exhibit the following qualities:

- Should be passionate about prayer.
- Should be known for regularly practicing prayer.
- Should have a humble heart.
- Should be growing in maturity in the Word and prayer.
- Should be one who is yielded and sensitive to the Holy Spirit.
- Should demonstrate sound wisdom and spiritual discernment.
- Should be merciful, compassionate and full of grace.
- Should be free of criticism, gossip, judgment, bitterness, and unforgiveness.
- Should have a strong faith and a willingness to learn.
- Should have a good reputation and be respected in the church and community.
- Should be able to lead and willing to follow.
- Most desirably, he/she should possess the qualities and attitude of a servant. Daniel Henderson says, "The true test of a servant is how he responds when he is treated like one."

Chapter 9
Policies, Procedures, and First Things

A key component of a successful summit is the establishment of Policies and Procedures. Once established, they can be used for future Prayer Summits hosted by your church.

The policies and procedures should be established by the Senior Pastor and the Prayer Summit Coordinator before the appointment of the Prayer Summit Committee. The policies should be reviewed before each Prayer Summit and modified to fit the particular summit. Much confusion and disagreement can be avoided if this practice is followed.

We will cover the policies that have proven to be helpful. Your church may wish to include others or may desire to modify these. They are not intended to be all-inclusive, but they should help you in establishing policies and procedures that fit your church.

POLICIES AND PROCEDURES

Attendance:
No part-time attendance will be allowed. Once registered on Wednesday, participants must stay the entire time. Participants are expected to attend all sessions, including small group gatherings. There will be no late arrivals, or leaving early.

Exceptions: Pastors or church leaders who must leave early to fulfill ministry duties.

Note: This time frame assumes a summit that begins on Wednesday evening and concludes on Saturday after lunch. This has proven to be an important policy because of the nature of entering into God's presence and the resulting transparency. Someone coming late disrupts the flow. They have not been present during the beginning instructional time and therefore do not know how to effectively participate. Incorrect conclusions may be drawn, and taken back to the church, doing damage through gossip. Leaving early is rude and disrespectful to the leaders and also disrupts the flow and short-circuits the time set aside in commitment to the LCPS.

Age limitations:
No attendees under the age of 19 years (must be out of High School). This includes babies and children with sitters or nannies.

Exceptions: None

Note: This requirement is due to the immaturity of most people under 19. The nature of transparency before God by adults, particularly during times of repentance or great brokenness, is not suitable for children or teenagers. Babies and children, even when accompanied by a sitter, are a disruption to their parents, the leaders, and others in attendance.

Eligibility for Attendance:
Attendance is limited to the local church body: either members or regular attendees. No guests or people from other churches are allowed.

Exceptions: Requests by Senior Pastor

Note: After you have hosted two or three summits for your congregation only, you may want to open the attendance to others. However, be careful that your church body comprises the major attendance. Otherwise, you no longer have a "local church" summit and dilute the benefits to your congregation. If you make the decision to allow attendance of others who are not from your church, keep the attendance at 85% your church body and 15% outsiders.

Summit Fee:
It is intended that the summit be self-supporting. Usually, there is not a financial allowance in the church budget for a Prayer Summit. Therefore, the fee for each summit attendee shall include reasonable allowances for marketing, mailing, printing, supplies, refreshments, honorariums, room fee reductions, and any other costs that are an-

ticipated. Pricing will be based on an estimated number of people expected to attend.

Once the pricing is determined, regardless of attendance, it should not be modified. If the amount collected is in excess of the expenses the difference should be set aside and earmarked for the next summit. If the amount collected is short of paying the summit expenses there should be an agreement that the church would pay the difference from the general budget.

Exceptions: None

Note: *The church may need to provide the original site deposit. It is a good idea to leave that deposit in your account, if you plan on future summits at that location.*

Registration Deposits:
At the time of registration, a deposit of one-half the total fee shall be required of each participant and is **non-refundable**. The deposit must be received before any room can be reserved.

The date for payment of the complete summit fee is usually one week before the commencement of the summit. Up until the final payment date, if the entire summit fee has been paid, one-half of the fee will be refunded upon cancellation. However, once the final payment date is announced there will be no **refunds** of any amount.

Exceptions: A request for a refund will be considered by the committee Finance Director at the time of request. If the reason for requesting a refund is due to circumstances beyond the control of the applicant, the request will be granted. But if the person simply changed his/her mind or states a similar reason, the request shall be denied.

Note: *Control of refunds is necessary because the site contract will specify a minimum number of attendees for which they will bill the Summit Committee, whether that minimum is met or not. In addition, all expenses of the summit will be determined by the anticipated number of attendees and distributed evenly to cover the expenses.*

Honorarium:
Full payment of the room/summit fee for the Primary Point Facilitator (usually the Senior Pastor) may be given. If this facilitator is

married, then the honorarium should include the full fee for the spouse as well. If there are children, an allowance not to exceed $200 may be included for childcare. The total honorarium is not to exceed $500.

Room Discount/Reduction:
Upon the decision of the committee, as an expression of appreciation, a room fee reduction of $50 per person may be offered to members of the pastoral or professional staff.

Note: The inclusion of this item is intended to encourage the staff and support people to attend the Prayer Summit. The Summit Committee should make the decision after consideration of the overall expected expenses of the Prayer Summit.

Bus/Transportation:
If the church has a bus, transportation may be provided for those who are unable to drive. The transportation cost shall be determined by the church and paid by each person using the transportation. The cost per person will be determined by dividing the total transportation cost by the number of seats available. The cost will be for a round trip. No refunds will be given if a person only rides one way. Payment will be collected in advance, and a boarding pass will be given at that time. No person will be able to ride without a boarding pass. Boarding passes may be transferred to another person.

Exception: Any exceptions will be decided by the committee.

Scholarships:
All scholarships will be limited to $50 per person, to be applied to the least expensive housing, usually a dormitory. In the case of a married couple, the amount may be applied to the least expensive double occupancy option. All scholarships will be covered by donations and will be available only as money becomes available. Both members and regular attendees may apply for a scholarship.[22] All requests for the $50 scholarship, in order to be considered, must include the balance of the summit fee. Consideration for individuals will be given on a first-come, first-served basis, according to the following criteria:

---

[22] A regular attendee is identified as having attended 4 of 6 Sunday church services within a two-month period.

- Has a legitimate need.
- Has been serving on the Summit Committee or at the Prayer Summit.
- Has never before attended a Prayer Summit.
- Those applying for a scholarship for the first time will be given priority.
- Is a member of the church.
- Is a regular attendee of the church.

Scholarship applications will be discontinued two weeks before commencement of the summit.

Offerings:
No requests for money or offerings will be taken at the Prayer Summit to cover any deficits, scholarships or any other financial need.

Exceptions: Pastor's decision

Disruptive People:
If there is any person at the Prayer Summit who is determined to be disruptive and a hindrance to the gatherings, either in the large group or a small group, after one warning they will be asked to leave and will be escorted off the premises. His/her registration fee shall be fully refunded. The pastor should assign this disciplinary responsibility to a staff member before the commencement of the summit.

Tenure of Prayer Summit Committee Members:
The Senior Pastor will appoint the Summit Coordinator and renew that appointment for each summit. The Summit Coordinator may serve for as many summits as the Sr. Pastor desires. The members of the Summit Committee will be appointed by the Summit Coordinator for a single summit. No member shall serve consecutively for more than two summits.

Exceptions: Pastor's decision

Note: Rotation of half the committee for each event is suggested to preserve continuity and to prevent having a completely new committee each time. The two-term tenure is designed to eliminate excessive ownership by a few. This tends to avoid the appearance of cliques and to bring in new people with a new sphere of contact and influence.

FIRST THINGS

In addition to determining the policies and procedures, there are several other items that need to be established by the Senior Pastor and Summit Coordinator before the Summit Committee begins.

Dates:
The date needs to be established before choosing a location. In order to give flexibility in the choice of a location, the Sr. Pastor and the Summit Coordinator should choose preferred and alternate dates. The final date will depend on the availability of the selected location. Because suitable sites often require a reservation somewhere between 9 and 12 months before the event, the choice of dates needs to be settled early.

Announce the date as soon as it is decided. Some people will need several months to make vacation arrangements with their place of employment. There are also other commitments that require people to have advance notice in order to make suitable arrangements to attend.

These dates should be selected and set aside, with instructions that no other church activity is to be planned for those dates. Remember that this is a LCPS for the entire adult church body, so it is wise to eliminate conflicts that might keep some from being able to attend.

Time Frame:
A Prayer Summit is generally scheduled for three to three and one half days. A good time frame is to begin the summit on a Wednesday evening after dinner (around 7:30 PM) and continue through Saturday after lunch (about 2:00 PM). This may seem like a long time; however, consider that it takes most people a full day to leave the cares of the world behind and to truly focus on the Lord. To experience the full blessing of God's presence at a Prayer Summit takes extended time. Most people spend more time than this regularly in frivolous activities, so we should not be shy about asking for this commitment of time to seek the presence of the Lord.

Location:
The Summit Coordinator, along with the Publicity Director, Room Assignment Supervisor and Finance Director,[23] should seek a suit-

---

[23] These positions and job duties are described in Chapters Ten and Eleven

The Power of a Prayer Summit   61

able location for the Prayer Summit. This process should begin somewhere between 12 to 15 months before your summit date. The final choice of location should then be submitted to the pastor for approval, and his signature on the contract provided by the site location.

The selection of the location for the summit is extremely important and should be suitable to your church. Be careful to select a location that is affordable, even if it does not have "hotel-type" accommodations. Remember, this is not intended to be a luxury vacation. If you determine that your church is too small to host a LCPS by itself, consider partnering with another church in your vicinity.

You might consider both secular and Christian conference sites. Some Catholic retreat centers will allow this type of meeting. Christian camps or retreat centers may be suitable. A small hotel that has conference accommodations might work. You might even consider a combination of overnight accommodations and a church for meetings in the location chosen.

A suitable location needs to include the following:

- A cost that fits the economics of your church.
- A location that provides for handicapped people.
- A large meeting room that can accommodate the number expected to attend and allow free space for standing and walking. You need a space that will allow a circular setup of the chairs with kneeling room between chairs and rows. The space should be large enough to allow room for the setup of prayer stations[24] during communion time. If you plan for an attendance of 120, the room should be able to accommodate 200–250.
- Enough smaller, private rooms to accommodate the small groups. These rooms should not be overly large in order to encourage intimacy. For a registration of 120, you will need four or five private rooms that each can accommodate 25 to 30 people.
- Overnight accommodations that will allow all attendees to stay together under one roof, in one location. There should be accommodations available for single occupancy, double occupancy, and dormitory-type occupancy, with pricing set

---

[24] For explanation and resources, see Appendix H.

accordingly. A large community area is desirable for social interaction during times when the summit is not in session.
- A location that provides and serves all meals in a dining area large enough to accommodate the entire group together. If your choice of location does not include the provision of meals, you may need to consider a caterer.
- A surrounding area that is conducive to outdoor activity, such as walking or sitting quietly alone.
- A location that is approximately one and one half to two hours away from your church. A distance farther than this tends to discourage attendance. However, any less tempts people to leave and travel back and forth from home. An important part of the blessing of a Prayer Summit is the extended time spent with one another and the bonding that takes place. Traveling back and forth does not allow one to leave the cares of the world behind and distracts both them and others from the overall summit environment of intimacy.

Be creative. Remember, this is not about the location or accommodations. It is about spending extended time seeking God's face together. You know your church. Select a location that will allow the most people in your congregation to attend. God wants to meet with you. If none of these suggestions meet your particular church's needs, pray!! God will show you a way.

Planning Schedule

Before the first Summit Committee meeting, to be held approximately six months before the summit date, all committee positions should be filled. A planning schedule[25] should be prepared by the Summit Coordinator to act as a guide to keep everyone on track. Be sure that the pastor has a copy of this schedule and all revisions. This schedule should be given to each person holding a committee position and should include meeting dates and contact information for each committee member.

---

[25] See Appendix D for a sample.

CHAPTER 10
THE SUMMIT COMMITTEE

When formulating the Prayer Summit Committee, it can be overwhelming and difficult; however, it is important to keep in mind the incredible blessings that flow as a result of participating in the planning of the Prayer Summit. Pray and think about people that might be interested in sharing in this experience, even if you do not know them well. Here are the testimonies of some Summit Committee members.

Anne, from Grace Church in Eden Prairie, Minnesota, describes being asked to serve on the Prayer Summit Planning Committee as "a blessing beyond words," and states that "my heart jumped with eagerness." She goes on to share:

> *We did what we could as far as the logistics go, but we simply trusted and praised Him for what He was going to do. We did not always know what to do–we were learning on the job–but we knew that this was God's work and that He would faithfully show us much grace.*
>
> *The joy of serving begins with the fellowship, love, and unity that the committee members develop for one another. Receiving phone calls from those who had questions about the Prayer Summit was one of the greatest unexpected blessings in preparation for the summit.*
>
> *Praying for them over the phone during those months, weeks, and days leading up to the prayer summit left me with a love and anticipation for what our Great God would do. I could*

clearly see that God was working long before the actual date of the summit.

During the summit, not only did I experience God's presence and power working in my own life, but I also experienced tremendous joy while serving, in seeing His people respond to Him in worship, trust, surrender, and also in seeing them blessed by His presence as He touched each person in the area of their deepest need.

Greg and Jennifer served on the Summit Committee at Arcade Church in Sacramento, California, for several years. Jennifer says:

When I was asked to be a part of the Prayer Summit Planning Committee, I was very intimidated at the idea of being with all those 'mighty prayer warriors.' Besides, I had never been on a committee, and did not know what to expect. I thought I would just go and not say anything, but simply listen and learn. I felt I really did not have much to offer, but my heart's desire was to serve the Lord so, I said yes to serving on the committee.

We spent a great deal of time praying and seeking the Lord before we began the committee meetings. The meetings always went smoothly. We'd discuss the financial struggles or other deterrents that would keep people from attending, and we'd lift these concerns before the Lord in prayer. I cannot remember one request that was not answered. It was amazing to see people give financially so that others could attend. A highlight was hearing the encouragement from past attendees to those who were apprehensive about going.

One of my favorite parts, as a committee member, was receiving the registration list before the summit, and having the opportunity to pray over each person, week after week. I'll never forget praying for a man that wanted to attend the summit but was having a difficult time making a commitment to go. He eventually overcame his inner struggles and registered, but with some resistance. When he arrived at the summit, he was full of anger. However, he left that Prayer Summit, at peace; a changed man. To this day, he walks closer with the Lord because he attended that summit.

What an awesome privilege we, the committee, had to pray that he would recognize the Lord's presence at that summit. Considering the opposition with which he was warring before the event, it is possible he may not have stayed at the summit if the committee had not prayed for him as we did.

I believe the most important activity of the Planning Committee was saturating the people with our prayers and inviting the Lord's presence into every facet of the summit, before it ever happened.

Not only did the committee pray for all who registered, but we spent a day at the facility in advance of the Prayer Summit. We prayed over the grounds, each and every room, the chairs, and the dining room; the whole place was prayed over inside and out.

Let the testimony of these people be an encouragement to you; do not be reluctant to ask people to serve on the committee. Be assured that it will be a positive experience, with great blessing for each one who participates in planning the LCPS.

FORMING THE PLANNING COMMITTEE

The Summit Coordinator should complete the appointment of committee members five to six months before the LCPS date. The Publicity Chairman, Room Assignment Chairman, and the Finance Chairman should be appointed earlier so they can participate in locating and choosing a summit location.

The suggested number of positions on the Planning Committee is twelve,[26] including the Summit Coordinator. The number of positions will vary according to each church's vision, so this number will differ from church to church. There is no question that a LCPS could be successfully planned by far less people if one looks only at duties. And certainly, for a very small church, less than twelve might be necessary.

One reason for having a larger Planning Committee is so that the members may also participate in the summit and not feel burnt out

---

[26] Some positions should be shared by a husband and wife. As a result, the total number of people can be more than twelve.

by the time and energy spent in planning the Prayer Summit. Another reason for a large committee is the desire that the congregation take ownership of the LCPS. It should not be perceived as an activity that is generated and planned by the pastor, church, staff, or a selected few who are always up-front in planning church activities. A large committee will have a bigger sphere of contact and influence than would be possible with just a few people. A bigger influence will generate a wider spread of enthusiasm within the congregation for attending the LCPS.

An additional benefit of a large group occurs when each meeting is begun with worship-based prayer. It encourages willingness to participate in, learn about, practice, and experience corporate Scripture reading, singing and prayer. This is one way of teaching worship-based prayer to the LCPS Committee members who are key people, and who in turn will influence others by modeling and will be able to participate with confidence at the LCPS.

Qualities of the Summit Committee Members:

- Should have a servant's heart and be willing to sacrifice time and effort.
- Sensitivity to what God is doing in the lives of people with whom they come in contact is helpful.
- The gift of hospitality is desirable.
- Should be people who have a heart for prayer and a desire to draw closer to the Lord.
- Should be able to complete tasks.
- Creativity is desired, yet not required.
- Should be friendly and of good reputation.

COMMITTEE POSITIONS
Here is a list of all the committee positions:

- Summit Coordinator
- Communion and Supply Supervisor
- Finance Director
- Publicity Director
- Recorder and Prayer Support Guide
- Refreshment Supervisor
- Registrar and On-Site Host

- Room Assignment Supervisor and On-Site Host
- Scholarship Support
- "Seek" Book Supervisor
- Small Group and Facilitator Coordinator
- Transportation and Pre-Trip Supervisor

Chapter 11
Committee Job Descriptions

The Summit Committee should start meeting as a group approximately five months before the summit date and should continue to meet once a month until the last month, when they should meet twice. One of the meetings during the last month can be the pre-trip to the site.

Some specific committees may want to meet before the first formal committee meeting to address time-sensitive needs. Those locating a site, as well as the Finance Committee, should meet as early as needed to secure a site and establish a budget. Training of the facilitators should begin approximately six months before the summit date. This timeframe may seem like it's too far in advance, but be assured that the time will go faster than you think.

It should be understood that each committee person is encouraged to involve other people in the performance of the duties assigned to them. These additional people will not be a part of the committee or sit in on the meetings, but they are valuable in their assistance, the widening of acceptance, and in creating the desire among the congregation to attend the summit.

The Summit Coordinator will conduct the meetings, act as a resource for each committee member, keep things running smoothly and on target, and will act as problem solver and liaison. General job descriptions are as follows:

Prayer Summit Coordinator:
(refer to Chapter Eight)

- Responsible for overall plans for the LCPS.
- Act as liaison between pastor, church staff, committee, and site personnel.
- Assist Senior Pastor in choosing and training facilitators.
- Participate with pastor in choosing the dates and time frame and in establishing Policies and Procedures.
- Participate with Finance Director preparing a budget for the summit and in setting the summit fee.
- Participate with pastor, Publicity Director, Room Assignment Supervisor, and Finance Director in locating a site for the Prayer Summit.
- Visit site, determine suitability for the LCPS, reserve the facility and gather all site contracts and paperwork for signatures.
- Become acquainted with site staff and develop a rapport with them.
- Participate with Finance Director in approval of final billing by site personnel.
- Prepare planning schedule and determine committee meeting place and dates.
- Appoint committee members and give job descriptions.
- Work closely with Publicity Director to determine the publicity needs, the type of publicity desired and the timeframe for release of the publicity.
- Oversee the creation of the "Seek His Face" Prayer Summit Guide.
- Conduct committee meetings.
- Be available to all committee members for help, advice, and problem solving.
- Handle or supervise all communications.
- Meet with the Senior Pastor often and keep him informed on the planning process.
- During the summit, act as on-site coordinator, host and problem solver.
- After the Prayer Summit prepare the final report for the Senior Pastor.

Note: The Senior Pastor is not a part of the committee, but he should be welcomed any time he'd like to attend a committee meeting. It is wise to ask him to attend the first committee meeting to show approval, give support, and generate enthusiasm.

Communion and Supply Supervisor

- Determine the number of people who will be attending the summit and the number of times communion may be served. Based on these numbers, purchase and/or assemble communion supplies.
- See that all basic supplies related to communion are gathered:

   a. tablecloths
   b. candles, matches and other table decorations
   c. containers for the bread and wine
   d. kneeling cushions
   e. boxes of tissues
   f. wastebaskets

- Check with the Summit Coordinator and the pastor to determine any other supplies that might be needed, such as a cross, prayer stations, foot washing supplies, paper for notes, etc.
- At the summit, see that communion elements are available when and where needed.
- At the summit, set up the room for communion, according to the pastor's instructions, when he schedules the corporate communion.
- Set up any other communion requests by the pastor.
- Afterward, clean up and return the area to its previous settings.
- Check with Planning Committee for supplies, besides communion supplies, that are needed and gather them together.

   a. chorus/hymn books
   b. "Seek His Face" Prayer Summit Guide
   c. tissues for meetings. (See that tissues are placed in appropriate locations.)

- Arrange for transporting all supplies to summit site.

Finance Director

- Responsible for collecting all money from registration, scholarship, or any other sources. This money should be deposited in an account set up by the church, requiring the signature of church finance personnel on all checks for payment of expenditures. All requests for money should be given in writing to the Finance Director, who when he approves the request will direct church finance personnel to write the check.
- Participate with the Summit Coordinator in the establishment of a budget.[27]
- Coordinate with Summit Coordinator in establishing the contract and the term therein, with the site personnel, before presenting it to the pastor for signature.
- Responsible for monthly reports of the Prayer Summit account to Summit Coordinator.
- Watch over the scholarship account and participate with Scholarship Support in determining and awarding scholarships.
- Participate with the Summit Coordinator in the establishment of the summit fee. The amount of this fee will depend on the budget that is set up for the summit.
- Look over and confirm the accuracy of the final billing from summit site personnel and see that the bill is paid in a timely manner.
- Work with the Summit Coordinator in preparing the final summit report for the pastor.

Publicity Director

- Prepare all publicity, including the following materials:

    a. Registration brochures and forms
    b. Posters
    c. Material for bulletin inserts
    d. Signs and flyers

- Create and monitor the registration website.
- Provide maps and directions to site.
- Arrange for announcements and testimonies from the pulpit.

---

[27] See Appendix E for sample budget and pricing.

The Power of a Prayer Summit 73

- Arrange for all printing needs.
- Arrange for all mailings.

Recorder and Prayer Support Guide

- Arrange for a Prayer Facilitator (on rotating basis) for committee meetings.
- Provide written prayer requests for the committee.
- Provide written prayer guide of summit-related requests to committee members on a monthly basis.
- Provide schedule and prayer guides for committee pre-summit trip.
- Record business minutes of committee meetings and give a copy to each committee member and the pastor. Keep extra copy for records.
- Before each meeting, obtain a list of the people registered for the summit from the Registrar, make copies, and see that each committee member has a copy for prayer.
- Attend to all written communication.

Refreshment Supervisor

- If needed or desired, arrange for coffee makers, cups, spoons, napkins etc. to be used at the summit. You may need to take them with you.
- If desired, provide light refreshments to be available at the summit "round the clock" such as coffee, tea, bottled water, cookies, crackers and nuts. During the winter and cold months, cough drops and cold remedies (aspirin etc.) are appreciated.
- Arrange for refreshments to be transported to the summit site.
- If desired, see that refreshments are ready at the committee meetings.
- Provide all clean-up of refreshment areas.

Registrar and On-site Host

- Responsible for all registration prior to summit, including on-line registration.
- Arrange for help at registration tables weekly, on the Sundays at the church before the summit.

- Receive and account for all money received for registration, including the following:

  a. Deposits
  b. Balance of fees
  c. Donations for scholarships

- Act as on-site greeter and host, with Room Assignment Supervisor, arriving early at the summit site to assure that each person is checked in and receives registration packet.
- Participate in the preparation and assembling of registration packet, containing:

  a. Welcome letter and emergency contact information
  b. "Seek His Face" Prayer Summit Guide
  c. Name badge
  d. Song/chorus book [28]
  e. Small group assignment
  f. Room assignment
  g. Site map

Room Assignment Supervisor and On-Site Host

- Assigns rooms according to the accommodation choice at registration of single occupancy, double occupancy or quad occupancy.
- Coordinates roommate choices.
- Arrange for any special handicap needs for rooms and/or transportation on summit grounds.
- Prepare name badges with room and small group identification.
- Act as on-site host and greeter with Registrar.
- Before sign-in, conduct last-minute room checks for any changes that may need to be arranged.
- Participate in final accounting with Finance Director and Summit Coordinator before payment of site bill.

Scholarship Support

- Participate with Summit Coordinator and pastor in establishing guidelines for awarding scholarships.

---

[28] See Appendix H.

The Power of a Prayer Summit   75

- Discuss requests for donations in the bulletin and from the pulpit with Publicity Director.
- Determine, with Finance Director and Summit Coordinator, eligibility for scholarship.
- Cooperate with Finance Director in keeping records of money available and money given for scholarships.
- With Recorder, arrange for thank-you notes to be sent to all donors to the scholarship fund.
- With Recorder, arrange for confirmation notices to be sent to those who have been approved for a scholarship.
- Keep a permanent record of recipients of scholarships.

"Seek His Face" Prayer Summit Guide[29] Supervisor

- Prepare, or make arrangements for someone else to prepare the "Seek His Face" Prayer Summit Guide:

    o   Print the books
    o   Assemble them

- Arrange for all facilitators to have a copy two weeks before the summit.
- Make arrangements for transporting the books to the summit site.

Small Group and Facilitator Coordinator

- Participate with pastor and Summit Coordinator in choosing facilitators.
- Arrange training for facilitators with the pastor.
- Participate with pastor and Summit Coordinator to determine the number of small groups.
- Assign facilitators and participants to the small groups.
- Give small group assignments to Room Assignment Supervisor for identification on name badges.

---

[29] See Appendix H. This book, called the "Seek His Face" Prayer Summit Guide is a reference to God's command in Psalm 27:8: "Seek My face." It is a book that contains material to help the attendees at the summit in worship and prayer. It is also designed to be taken home and used in their personal daily time seeking God's face after the summit.

Transportation and Pre-Trip Supervisor

- Arrange group transportation to the summit site for pre-trip.
- Arrange transportation to the summit for the attendees, if transportation is to be provided; a bus is ideal.
- Make sure a bus driver is available for both the pre-trip and the summit. Reserve his services.
- Determine the transportation fee.
- Work with Publicity Director to have boarding passes prepared.
- Collect transportation fee from each person.
- Give fees to Finance Director.
- See that all information regarding the pre-trip is given to each committee member, facilitators, and the pastor.
- Make arrangements with summit site personnel for the transportation of handicapped people around the grounds, from meeting room to meeting room, and to the dining room.

These descriptions of job duties are informative as to details that need to be addressed in planning a LCPS. However, this is only a guide and should be adjusted to the needs of your church.

PART III

Preparing For The Summit

Chapter 12
Preparing the Congregation

Viruses live wherever there is life. They cannot live or grow outside a host cell. They are very contagious, and their purpose is to infect every living thing with which they come in contact. Their shape varies from simple to complex, and there is an incubation time before the infection is noticeable.

Wisely used, the preparation time before a LCPS can be a time of incubation for *"infection of the affections,"* through exposure to corporate, Spirit-led, and worship-based prayer. This infection can act like a virus and be highly contagious, infecting every living thing, whether their understanding of prayer is simple or complex.

Pastor Earl Heverly of Sacramento, California, has not determined a date for a LCPS yet. He states that he has been introducing Spirit-led, worship-based prayer to his congregation through prayer times in small group meetings and the weekly "Experiencing the Spirit" prayer meeting. Because all of his staff participates, they will be prepared and comfortable with this format of prayer; they will be a great asset when the time is right for their LCPS.

Pastor Todd Eenigenburg of West Chicago, Illinois is also preparing his congregation through Spirit-led, worship-based prayer. He says:

> *We are taking the beginning steps toward re-educating people on the purpose and focus of prayer. I have begun to lead prayer gatherings that focus on seeking God's face. People are very positive towards this approach. Some say it feels like*

what church should be about. People now enjoy the opportunity to participate and to pray together.

These congregations have been infected and are in the incubation period. There are many positive results a church can experience by taking an extended time to teach, and provide exposure to, worship-based prayer before hosting a LCPS. However, it is not a necessity. Many people get their first exposure at a Prayer Summit.

It is wise to provide some preparation to the congregation before they attend the summit. Many churches are not practicing corporate prayer, and so they have lost the value of praying together. If there is a corporate prayer gathering, it is often a group of women or another small group, led by a lay person, not the pastor who should be leading by example.

Pastors Vroegop, Eenigenburg and Heverly all agree that it is important that corporate prayer, including both men and women, is practiced regularly and led by the pastor. Pastor Todd Eenigenburg says, "Whatever a church says is important should have the participation and leadership of the pastor." Vroegop states:

> We pastors are called to lead in the Word and prayer. If our people don't see us leading the corporate prayer gathering of the church, they will assume that prayer is not important. It is no different than saying we should have the Word of God as the central thing that defines our lives, but then never talk about the Word.

> So, my ministry has to be the word and prayer. If all I do is talk about prayer, but there is no actual time of prayer or a place where the church prays, then people hear about prayer, but they don't see prayer practiced. So, it doesn't connect.

He goes on to question:

> Where is the 'hub' for the church prayer time, a family meal so to speak–where is that? Many can tell me where that is for their Sunday morning celebration around the word, but in terms of prayer it is often lacking. There is no designated time.

The announcement that the church will host a LCPS is a perfect time to challenge, prepare, and teach the congregation to look at prayer differently than the prevalent need-based practice. It can be a time of leading people into a wonderful experience of Spirit-led prayer that brings them into the presence of God as they focus their worship on God's character, rather than on what He does or what they want Him to do.

Pastor Earl says, "The supernatural manifestations of God's presence should mark Christian gatherings as demonstrated in the New Testament. The characteristics of the Kingdom of Heaven should always permeate our gatherings, rather than being the exception."

The key phrase is "Christian gatherings," not just for the prayer summit gathering, but also all the church gatherings. Preparation for the LCPS can be the prelude that begins the process of experiencing the supernatural manifestation of God's presence regularly in every Christian gathering.

About six months before the summit date, around the same time training begins for the Prayer Facilitators, the pastor should begin a sermon series on prayer. The series should stress the corporate side of prayer and the value of praying together. This is a valuable introduction to the LCPS whether it is your first summit or not. It sets the stage and sends the message that this is a very important event[30].

In connection with the sermon series, set up times for corporate prayer where Spirit-led, worship-based prayer can be modeled and invite the congregation to participate. Since you will be training Prayer Facilitators at this time, it is advantageous to provide opportunities for them to practice what they're learning.

To encourage participation, consider a focus such as "40 days of prayer," using a prepared prayer guide with daily or weekly corporate prayer scheduled. The newly trained facilitators can lead these times of prayer. At the conclusion of the 40 days, have an evening of corporate prayer led by the pastor featuring prayer stations[31] and testimonies.

---

[30] Refer to Daniel Henderson, *Fresh Encounters*, Chpt. 10-11. Also, see Resources for information on ordering a copy.
[31] See Appendix H.

Providing opportunities to learn about and to practice Spirit-led, worship-based prayer before the summit will begin the *"infection of the affections."* As a result, the desire to attend the LCPS will be strong, and infected hearts will be prepared to experience a powerful encounter with God as they participate at the LCPS. However, be careful that the summit is not regarded as "the end." It should be the beginning. If the LCPS is thought of primarily as a church event, activity or program—something to attend for personal or spiritual pleasure—the goal of changing the prayer DNA in all ministries of the church to Spirit-led worship-based will be lost.

The LCPS should be regarded as a tool for the introduction of a pathway to experiencing the presence of God through worshiping together, listening for and following the Spirit, and seeking God for who He is and not what He does. It should be the beginning of a new prayer culture in the church.

Chapter 13
Facilitator Preparation

The biggest challenge at the beginning for the Prayer Facilitators is to look at prayer differently than the commonly accepted need-based paradigm. Listening for and hearing the voice of God and the Holy Spirit before proceeding may be foreign and threatening to a facilitator's style of leadership. Being comfortable with silence is often a problem. And yet, understanding, acceptance and practice of the components of seeking direction from the Holy Spirit before proceeding, hearing the voice of God, and practiced silence is critical to a Prayer Facilitator's assignment at a Prayer Summit.

Although the focus of this section is on the pastor preparing and teaching facilitators, he should not neglect his own preparation for the summit. He will be the Primary Point, and much of what is stated here and what he will teach applies to the Primary Point of the summit.

Preparation of the facilitators includes both teaching and providing them with opportunities where they can practice. They should start practicing two months after training starts and continue to do so until the summit. Therefore, identifying facilitators should begin shortly after the pastor commits to hosting a LCPS. It is best to schedule only the facilitators together first; then, as they become comfortable with worship-based prayer, others from the congregation can be included.

The Prayer Facilitators should include what they are learning in their personal time with the Lord by incorporating the worship-based elements as well as listening for and responding to God's voice.

Focusing on an attribute of God, praying Scripture, and singing choruses that relate to that attribute are good places to start.

Praying through a Psalm a day is also a good place to start. For instance, in Psalm 91 one will find God's attributes of Shelter, Refuge, Deliverer, Protector, and Provider. He is also described as Almighty and Faithful. Prepare material that you might use at a summit in response to the themes of this Psalm. Steep yourself in Scripture that helps you focus on God's face at the summit.

Practice silence before God. Make plans for extended time alone with the Lord in prayer, fasting, and confession before the summit. It is helpful to spend this time away from home and familiar surroundings.

One of the defining characteristic of a Prayer Summit is that there is no "agenda." The Holy Spirit is the leader, and we follow where He leads. This does not mean we should not be prepared. God has much to say about preparing. His instructions to Aaron and his son as priests were quite extensive and complete. This included their personal preparation as well as how they were to approach God on behalf of the people.[32] Not having an agenda *does* mean we listen for the Holy Spirit's leading by identifying themes that occur over and over and that we are flexible and ready to follow Him.

Do not neglect your preparation. Even though there is no agenda, there is a need to be prepared. The Holy Spirit cannot use what we do not know. Therefore, have a list of Scripture passages, hymns, and choruses identified by theme to be used in response to the Holy Spirit's leading.

Themes of God's faithfulness, forgiveness, majesty, glory, wonder, and holiness are typical. As you focus on a particular prayer theme, use accompanying scripture and songs that are an enhancement to the theme. Keep it vertical.

When people worship and praise God, a response occurs because people recognize their unworthiness before a Holy God. Often, confession occurs. This is the time to be prepared with scriptures and songs that address unforgiveness, fear, trust, God's love and acceptance, insecurity, God's forgiveness, and God's provision.

---

[32] Exodus 28,29 and Leviticus 8-9 NKJV

Do not run ahead of the Spirit. Listen for His leading and follow Him. It takes time to learn how to listen for His leading. This is a very important facet of learning and practice, before the summit, in preparation for facilitating at the summit.

In Chapter Eight we discussed the role of the Prayer Facilitator team. We stated that the facilitating team is usually made up of three people, one who is identified as the Point, and two assistants. The facilitating teams should be identified well before the date of the summit.

Approximately four months before the summit, the Point of each team should take the lead in scheduling time for the team to worship and pray together weekly until the summit. Each team should meet together once a week for three weeks of each month. During the fourth week of each month, all facilitators of every team should meet together with the pastor. This should be a time of practicing Spirit-led, worship-based prayer as well as sharing with and supporting each other.

The goal of the facilitator is to help the participants in a vertical interaction with God. Unconfessed sin, lack of preparation, lack of personal worship (during personal time and at the summit), a lack of familiarity with appropriate music, a lack of building the facilitator team, a lack of being connected to the moment, and a lack of listening to the Holy Spirit are all hindrances to a Spirit-led time of worship.

Chapter 14
Preparation of the Summit Site

I know of a woman with five children who feels like she always has a messy house and never has time to prepare properly, clean, or pick up the clutter when company is expected. This is especially stressful when the guest is "important."

She has developed a way to alert everyone that immediate preparation needs to take place for the expected important guest. She shouts, "Take Five!" The entire family stops what they are doing and joins her in preparing for the guest's arrival. This plan assures a proper welcome for the important one.

Before the Passover meal we call "The Last Supper," Jesus said to Peter and John:

> "Go and **prepare** the Passover for us, that we may eat." So they said to Him, "Where do You want us to **prepare**?" And He said to them, "Behold, when you have entered the city, a man will meet you carrying a pitcher of water; follow him into the house which he enters. Then you shall say to the master of the house, 'The Teacher says to you, where is the guest room where I may eat the Passover with My disciples?' Then he will show you a large, furnished upper room; there **make ready.**" So they went and found it just as He had said to them, and they **prepared** the Passover.[33] *(Emphasis added)*

What guest could be more important than God Himself? The entire purpose of a LCPS is to meet with the Important One. Therefore, the

---
[33] Luke 22:8-12 NKJV

place of meeting needs to be cleaned up, picked up, and *prepared*. It is time for the entire planning committee and all the facilitators to stop what they are doing and *Take Five!!* We call this the pre-trip. The date, time, and other arrangements should be given to all committee members and facilitators with the instructions that their attendance is strongly encouraged. Remember that special arrangements may need to be made at the site and/or by the committee, so as much notice on the trip details is ideal as the attendance of everyone at this pre-trip is desired. Generally, the pastor does not need to attend; however, an invitation should be extended to him.

There are several goals for the pre-trip:

1. To make a last minute check of arrangements and accommodations.
2. To become acquainted with site personnel, grounds and surrounding area.
3. To receive requirements and regulations from the summit personnel.
4. To arrange for any special requirements or needs.
5. To spend time together in thanksgiving and worship before the commencement of the summit.
6. To prepare for the presence of our "important" guest by praying over all areas that will be used for the summit.

If at all possible, travel to the site as a group. Part of the blessing of this trip is the time together on the trip. Keep this in mind as you plan meals around the site visit. Possibly arrive just a little before lunch and enjoy a bag lunch together and/or leave around dinnertime and share dinner together at a restaurant.

When you arrive, the Summit Coordinator should meet with the site personnel and confirm that all arrangements are in place. The following tasks should be done on the pre-trip:

1. Provide instructions as to how you want both the large gathering room and the small group rooms set up.

   (The meeting rooms, for both the large group and the small groups, should have the seating arranged in a circular pattern. In the large group, there should not be more than three rows of chairs. In the small groups, one row only is most ef-

fective. The chairs should not be crowded, but should allow space for comfortable movement and kneeling. Several aisles, evenly spaced, should be provided. Place a small box of tissues on the floor between every six to eight chairs.

The inner circle circumference, for the large group, should surround an empty space of about 18 X 18 feet. On communion night, this area should be increased to about 25 feet by 25 feet to allow the communion table to be placed in the center of the circle and still allow plenty of room for movement.

If a public address system will be needed, make sure it will be in place or confirm that you need to provide one yourself.)

2. Check the provisions for people who may have disabilities.
3. Check the lodging that has been assigned to you.
4. Check the site schedule for meals.
5. Confirm arrival and departure times for the summit.
6. Take time to conduct a prayer tour. Appoint one of the facilitators to be the Point and direct the focus of prayer. Begin with a time of worship together, somewhat like a "mini"-prayer summit. The focus at this pre-summit prayer is certainly on who God is, but we also want to ask for His blessing on what He will do at the prayer summit.

Spend time in confession, praying for each other, the church and the pastor. Spend time entreating God to be present at the summit and for the Holy Spirit to lead.

From there, you can break up into smaller groups or stay together. Have a list of the people who have registered and pray for each one by name. If not occupied, pray in each of the rooms that the small groups will use as well as the large group meeting area. Spiritual warfare type prayers are appropriate. Walk the grounds and pray for protection and a shield around the entire site.

Pray for all the site personnel. Pray for the people who will not be attending, but will be at home. Pray for protection for the pastor and the facilitators. End the time praying for the facilitators.

Enjoy this time together with God. Follow where God leads you on this pre-trip and prepare to be blessed.

PART IV

Convening The Summit

Chapter 15
Leading the Large Combined Group

God likes parties, celebrations, and feasts. As the people gather for the first meeting at the LCPS, there is definitely an atmosphere of celebration and expectation. There is a pervading party mood. There is a sense of waiting for something to happen or someone to appear.

THE FIRST MEETING
This first meeting is a time when the structure of the summit is set forth. Explain that there is no agenda; however, there is a schedule and a focus. It is helpful to remind them of the difference. An *agenda* is a list of items or matters to be discussed or dealt with. It includes a predetermined list of things to be done. The *schedule*[34] is simply a timetable listing the time of the meetings and the meals to enable order and compliance with the needs and requirements of the site personnel. A *focus* is a single point of interest or activity; it is the center of activity. The Prayer Summit focus is singular: to seek God for who He is. Everything is subject to change by the Holy Spirit.

Give acknowledgments, introductions and housekeeping details. Discuss the schedule, making sure it is clear and understood. Give thanks to those who planned and prepared the summit. Request a fast from phone use (and other electronic devices). Ask that all attendees leave cell phones in their cars or another safe place so that they will not be used during the summit. This request should include the time when they are not in meetings as well as when they are.

---
[34] See Appendix G for a sample schedule

The Prayer Summit is a time set aside to be separated from the cares and distractions of people and circumstances which are not of an emergency nature. Communication is to be limited to God and each other. Ask them to provide the site emergency phone number to anyone who may need to contact them. Make known and emphasize the requirement of their attendance at all meetings.

This is the only time these things are openly discussed. The participants should be instructed who to contact for whatever further information or assistance they might need.

The Primary Point, usually the pastor, will introduce all the facilitators and explain their function. It should be announced that the summit is not intended to be a place for counseling, but that the facilitators are available to pray with anyone over anything that might be troubling them.

During the first meeting, give instruction regarding the focus of the Prayer Summit and how the summit will work. Explain that there are four basic elements to a Prayer Summit: prayer, singing, reading of Scripture, and personal response. Discuss group dynamics and the format of the groups. Go over the guidelines and stress the need for confidentiality.[35]

It is important that the format of seeking God's face (who He is) and not His hand (what He does) is explained and understood. Be sure to discuss the acceptability of silence, the importance of listening, and the need for acceptance of a variety of worship expressions by others.

Appendix F contains these guidelines, and you may find it helpful to read the guidelines in full at this first meeting so nothing is left undone. Include them in your "Seek His Face" Prayer Summit Guide so each person can refer to them as needed. To enhance people paying attention, consider different people reading each section of the guidelines.

The nature of the music should be acknowledged. We have found that the greatest impact seems to be experienced when there is no instrumental participation and the Prayer Summit Committee plans songs that will be sung a cappella. In an effort to keep distractions to a minimum, we suggest that you refrain from referencing song num-

---

[35] See Appendix F

bers and locations, rather encourage participants to sing along if they're familiar with the song, sit quietly and meditate on the words, or look inside their booklet if they would like to sing along.

Announce that after each meeting, all the facilitators will meet with the Primary Point. This announcement is made so no one is anxious when they observe this practice. The purpose of these meetings is for consensus in the direction the Holy Spirit is leading, for determination of the timing of breakouts into small groups, for encouragement, for prayer for each other, and for sharing experiences. All of this is to enhance the summit for all the participants.

As you can see, this first meeting sets the stage for the summit and gets details out of the way. If announcements need to be made at a later time, mealtimes are the best opportunity to do this.

After all the announcements and housekeeping details have been addressed, begin the worship. This is a time to praise God for bringing people together to seek His presence. It is a time to invite Him to be an active participant through leading all summit activity, as well as a time for each heart to surrender to His leading. It is a time to leave all cares and concerns behind.

Remember that the time for this first meeting is short and that people are tired. Do not linger for an excessive amount of time. Tomorrow, the journey into God's presence will begin.

THE SECOND MEETING

One pastor shared after facilitating his first LCPS:

> *The first time I facilitated at a Prayer Summit, I was overwhelmed. I had a sense of insufficiency and humility, which created an awareness of my need for absolute trust and dependence upon God, if anything of eternal value was going to be accomplished.*

I'm sure every first-time facilitator would say the same thing. After the summit, this same pastor said, "I never cease to be amazed by our great God."

At this early session of the summit, prepare to be overwhelmed, perhaps even somewhat panicked. For many, not having an agenda or a planned program is daunting. Yet, that is not your responsibility. The agenda and program is the responsibility of the Holy Spirit. When the enemy assails you with doubts, tell the Holy Spirit just that. You can be sure the Holy Spirit will not fail or leave you stranded.

Many facilitators say that the hardest part of facilitating is to know how to start. They feel that they have not heard clearly from the Spirit until the session is underway. So, how does one start?

Dennis Fuqua, who has led a number of Prayer Summits as Primary Point through International Renewal Ministries,[36] answers this way:

> *I always take time before each prayer session to prepare. During these times, I quiet my heart before Him and simply enjoy Him. This could be a very brief time of prayer or a more extended time.*
>
> *I ask the Lord if there is any specific direction He wants to take in this prayer session. My observation is that about two thirds of the time, I have some direction I believe is from the Lord. This might be in the form of a single word like 'grace' or 'thanksgiving,' or it could be in the form of a verse or passage of Scripture.*
>
> *The clarity of this direction is sometimes quite clear and direct. Other times it is just a nudge or a hunch. Often I simply begin the session without a clear sense of direction from Him. Sometimes when I think I have a direction from Him, and end up following that direction, the Spirit leads in a different direction. Obviously I have not heard clearly from the Spirit and have been following my direction not His. In these instances, because I am surrendered to the leading and direction of the Holy Spirit, He shows His desire and direction. A sensitivity to the Holy Spirit and a willingness to let Him lead are significant keys to facilitating."*

Begin with inviting the Holy Spirit to come and take over. Praying a prayer of invocation is valuable in preparing each heart for the presence and leading of the Holy Spirit. Use Scripture and songs that reinforce this request.

---

[36] For more information on International Renewal Ministries, visit www.PrayerSummits.net, or email Dennis Fuqua at Dennis@PrayerSummits.Net.

Move on in the journey into the throne room, recognizing the cloud of witnesses[37] that surround us, and perhaps joining the worship going on in Heaven.[38] Use your holy imagination. Use Scripture and songs that aid in entering into the presence of God or introduce any attribute of God. Be sure to listen to the responses of the participants; you will be able to know the leading and direction of the Holy Spirit. As people are prompted by the Holy Spirit to participate, you will hear a theme emerge. This is the leading of the Holy Spirit. Go with it!

As you respond to the direction and leading of the Holy Spirit, be creative as you encourage participation. God is creative. He is not dull. A good reference to read before facilitating at a summit, which will help in this area is *PRAYzing!, Creative Prayer Experiences from A to Z* by Daniel Henderson.[39]

As you lead, keep in mind the "4/4 Time"[40] pattern of prayer. Basically, the large group meetings are composed of the *Upward* stroke (reverence-worship). This is a time when worship is all about God. All praise and worship should be for who He is, not what He has done. A typical time in the large group might look like how one participant described it:

The responsibility of each person was simply to be sensitive to God's Spirit and His direction of worship. Right after we started praising and worshiping God, the countenances of many people began to change. Peace seemed to prevail. It was clear that God's Spirit was moving among us. As we sang songs such as, 'On Holy Ground,' the Holy Spirit was powerful in the room.

> *As I focused on God, I experienced Him in powerful ways, both individually and as one of the group. I forgot who was next to me; I focused on the Lord and had a sense of anticipation about what He would show me. As many Scripture passages were read, they took on a personal note, as if God was speaking to me personally.*
>
> *The facilitator read Scripture promises, and we were invited to stand and thank God for His promises as they applied to*

---

[37] Hebrews 12:1
[38] Revelation 4:8,11 NKJV
[39] See Resource section.
[40] See Appendix B.

> our life. The facilitator prompted participation in many ways, such as suggesting short prayers to God like, 'God I thank you for _____,' or 'God you are awesome in my life because _____,' or 'I love you Lord because _____.' The time progressed with spontaneous song, Scripture reading, and responses from the participants.
>
> A few times, we were given breaks, to allow for time of personal prayer and journaling. This personal time was very valuable to talk privately with God and to reflect on what He was revealing. The prayer summit provided me quality time to express my love for Him by seeking and focusing only on God.

As a facilitator, be aware of tiredness and exhaustion of the people, and give them breaks. Consider calling a time for personal reflection for everyone. Instruct them to take a walk and find a quiet place for personal meditation and journaling. Some may need to take a nap. Be sure that your instructions include the admonishment that this is not a time to visit or socialize. The time is to be spent with the Lord alone. You may want to call for a "Code of Silence."[41]

After some time, there will be a shift to the *Downward* stroke (response), as in, "Because of who He is how should I respond?" The large group meetings will focus mostly on the *Upward* and *Downward* stroke—areas of reverence, worship, and response.

When the theme turns consistently to the *Inward* stroke (requests, repentance, and forgiveness), it is time to break into small groups. This will probably not happen on your first day. Do not rush. Give plenty of time for worshiping God for who He is and for the fact that He is worthy of worship. Enjoy Him. Bask in His presence. Know His love. Commune passionately with Him; give Him your best praise and worship.

[ii] A "Code of Silence" is a time, specified by a facilitator, during which there is to be no talking—conversation, communication, or whatever—with others. The time is for silent meditation with the Lord.

Chapter 16
Leading the Small Group

One facilitator shared that when the announcement was made that it was time to go to the breakout groups, panic and intimidation arose within him. This was his first time facilitating, and he had been designated the point for his small group. Suddenly, he couldn't remember anything he had learned about worship-based prayer and facilitating. He was desperately afraid of failing, looking foolish, and being embarrassed, not just before the people in his group, but also before the other two facilitators assigned to his group.

Don't be surprised if you, as a facilitator, also have these emotional reactions. Remember, the enemy does not want anyone to seek God and experience His power. Therefore, he will do anything he thinks will defeat or hinder peace, healing, revival, and renewal that will take place in the small group. Foremost in your mind should be the realization that you are not the one leading and not the one responsible for anyone's response or what may be considered success. The Holy Spirit is the one who is in charge of the group, and you are only the vessel–the conduit–through which He will work. And He will work!

The small group differs in a number of ways from the large group. First, the groups are broken down by gender. By separating into gender-specific groups, individuals have more freedom to share and relate to the issues facing their peers. Even when couples attend, we still encourage men to meet and pray with men and women with women.

The focus of the small group is different from the large group. The large group focus is primarily one of recognizing the character of God, which results in reverence and elicits a response of praise, worship, and surrender. The large group's focus remains mostly in the first two strokes of the "4/4" pattern: *Upward* (reverence-worship) and *Downward* (response).The small group should always begin with the *Upward* stroke (reverence-worship), but it will quickly progress into the *Downward* stroke (response) and the *Inward* stoke (requests).

The response in the small group will be different than in the large group. While the response in the large group is largely praise and recognition of who God is, the response in the small group is one of recognizing our failings in light of who God is and thus, our need for confession, repentance, forgiveness, and renewal.

The room is set up slightly different than in the large group. The chairs are in a circle but in only a single row. In the center of the circle is either one chair or two empty chairs facing each other. Make sure there are plenty of tissues within easy reach of all chairs, including the center chairs.

There is a difference in the interaction of the participants also. Because of the more intimate setting, participants will from time to time be led to approach and pray with someone about a specific issue shared.

When the Point Person begins the small group, it is wise to set some boundaries. Start by introducing the other facilitators. Because the focus of the small group session is on prayer and worship, it is best to refrain from introductions and "get to know you" activities. Do stress the guideline, of Scripture reading, singing, and prayer, set forth in the first day's large group meeting. Do remind them that there is a need to follow the direction of the Holy Spirit. Do stress that the purpose of the small group is to seek God and to relate to Him, not to each other by offering, or seeking, advise, counseling or solutions to problems from one another. The center of attention should be God not any person. Therefore, all prayers and requests should be addressed to Him. Relay that the prayers are to be *personal*, not about someone they know, missionaries, or a prayer request someone has given them. Use Scripture and remind them that Jesus says:

Again I say to you that if two of you agree on earth concerning anything that they ask, it will be done for them by My Father in heaven. For where two or three are gathered together in My name, I am there in the midst of them.[42]

Note that even though Jesus is not visible to their eyes, He is faithful; therefore, He is present in the small group. Explain that the chairs in the middle of the circle represent the place where Jesus is sitting. Instruct them to either kneel at the feet of Jesus before the chair where He is sitting, or to sit in the chair opposite where Jesus is sitting, and talk to Him.

There is a tendency for people to tell each other their problems, issues, hurts, and distresses. Discourage that communication and instruct them to "Tell Jesus, and we will listen in." Also discourage people from rushing to pray for someone who is in emotional distress. They should give that person plenty of time to communicate with God.

As you begin the small group session with praise and worship, be sensitive to the leading of the Holy Spirit into areas of confession, repentance, and forgiveness. Use Scripture and songs that reinforce these areas. Fear, anger, lack of trust, and insecurity may all emerge during this time. It is wise to be prepared with Scripture passages, in these areas, that you can retrieve quickly.

The facilitating team should function together smoothly during this time. Perhaps, the Point will want to designate one of the facilitators to focus on Scripture passages and the other to focus on songs. Both should concentrate on listening to the Holy Spirit and the participants. Do not be shy about communicating among yourselves about what is going on or where you sense the Spirit is leading. Short notes, passed to each other are a good way to do this.

Don't be fearful of silence. God speaks in silence. You might even want to call for a few minutes (3–5) of silence. When silence naturally occurs, do not be like the small girl whose father heard her talking as he walked by her bedroom door. He could not make out what she was saying, so he opened the door and went in to listen. She was kneeling at her bedside, obviously praying. But she was

---

[42] Matthew 18:19-20 NKJV

only reciting the alphabet–A, B, C, D, E–and so forth, over and over. Finally, her father asked her what she was doing.

She replied, "Praying."

"But you weren't saying anything. Why were you just reciting the alphabet?"

"Well," she said, "I didn't know what to say, so I figured if I gave God the letters, He could make the words."

When silence comes, wait for the "words" from the Holy Spirit. He knows what you should say. One woman describes her experience at a LCPS in this way:

> *After a time in the large group, we left the worries and distractions of the world and began to focus on seeking God in a more personal way. We then broke into separate groups, limited to either all men or all women, of about 15 people each. The facilitators began our time in a variety of ways, usually with prayer and focusing on a particular attribute of God.*
>
> *In our small group, we had an opportunity to pray aloud about personal areas in which we each had needs. One person sought release from anger toward her parents. Another was facing a difficult situation in her marriage. Another was consumed with fear and anxiety. And another was ridden with guilt and unforgiveness. As they prayed, others in the group joined them and asked for God's healing and guidance. Regardless of the issue an individual faced, we witnessed God's miracle as He brought peace to each one. I really sensed Christ's presence. There was an incredible spirit of love apparent within the group, a spirit of both God's love and love for one another.*

After spending extended time in the presence of God at a Prayer Summit, the extravagant love of God calls us to sit at the feet of Jesus. Unresolved issues, unmet needs, unhealed hurts, painful results of sin, and an attitude of unforgiveness are all laid at His feet. And He is always faithful to meet and minister to each one, regardless of the need. Truly, this is a miracle–the miracle of God's unfathomable love.

Chapter 17
Communion

Dennis Fuqua shares:

> *Consistently, the deepest times of worship at a Prayer Summit seem to come around the communion table. When there aren't time constraints or other emphases, sharing in the broken body and shed blood of Jesus at a summit allows people to process the significance of the cross in a deeper way, which results in a deep love for and appreciation of Jesus as well as a deep sense of need for Him.*
>
> *The last evening of the Prayer Summit is different than the other times when the people have been together, either in the large group or in a small group. This service covers an extended period of time dedicated to communion. As in the large group, the men and women are together for the communion service. The service often lasts up to three hours. Although communion may have been enjoyed at other times during the summit, this communion service is different and is very special. It can be described as the "crescendo" of the entire summit.*
>
> *The inner circle of chairs is widened to accommodate a table, approximately eight feet long and four feet wide, with a space of about six feet all around the table. The table is covered with a white tablecloth. In the center of the table is a candelabrum. Also on the table, within easy reach from anywhere around the table and from both sides of the table, are trays of bread and wine (or juice).*

Keep the communion table simple. Remember, the focus is the bread, wine, and communion with Jesus, not a beautifully decorated table. The bread and wine should be the place where your eyes are drawn, not the decorations.

One suggestion is to use candlelight as the only form of lighting during communion. This said, there should be enough candles for adequate light. On the floor, around the base of the table, place several kneeling cushions. There should be waste containers in a convenient location to receive the used disposable wine cups. Make sure plenty of tissues are within easy reach of everyone.

Sometimes, prayer stations[43] are included as part of the communion setting to enhance worship, to help people realize the sacrifice of Jesus, to provide a place for confession of sin, and to give a way to express servanthood to one another.

At the beginning of the service, the candles are not lit, and the lights are on normal. The meeting begins, as other meetings do, with the *Upward* stroke of reverence and worship. The Scripture passages and songs should turn to the sacrifice of Jesus, forgiveness of sin, and God's love. Ask the participants to hold the Scripture passages and songs regarding the cross until communion has begun. Listen for the Holy Spirit's prompting that it is time to begin communion.

When you hear the Holy Spirit's prompting, usually by an emerging theme in the declared Scripture passages and songs, give instructions regarding communion. Make sure people understand that they are to go to the table when they are ready and take communion alone, with someone else, or even with several others. They can kneel at the table, find a quiet spot, or go back to their chairs; they can choose whichever they want. Express that there is plenty of time, so they can linger and enjoy the Lord's presence. Light the candles, turn off the lights, and prepare to meet the Lord.

Come with me and observe:

> *I enter the room, just after the candles are lit, in time to hear the facilitator say, "—do this in remembrance of Me.[44]" Immediately I feel the presence of the Lord. In the soft glow of*

---
[43] See Appendix H.
[44] Luke 22:19 NKJV

the candles, as I hear the beautiful voices singing in harmony, I am enveloped with peace. I stand back and just enjoy the glow that is over the entire room.

My eyes are drawn to the life-sized cross at the front of the room, softly lit with a spotlight. I notice that three people are kneeling at the foot of the cross, and they appear to be writing on something. As I watch, I can't help but notice the tears on the face of one and another's silent sobbing. Meanwhile, the third one picks up a hammer and nails a paper to the cross. Then, the other two do the same. The sound of that hammer connecting with the nails jars my peace and brings to my remembrance what the cross represents. I know that written on those papers are sins that have been confessed and then nailed to the cross, which represents where Jesus died for those sins.

I observe people, one by one, two by two, and sometimes in a small group, making their way to the table, where they kneel and pick up the bread and wine. They bow their heads in respect and reverence. They remember the sacrifice of Jesus as they pray and eat the bread representing His body and drink the wine representing His blood. All of their faces seem to have a soft light about them.

As I look to the left, I see a small table with a bowl of red liquid, a cross, small stones, and markers. A man comes to this table, picks up a stone, writes something on it, and places it in the liquid. He kneels in front of the table, obviously praying. I continue to look at the stone, now in the liquid, and I see that whatever he wrote is disappearing from the stone. I read the sign on the table and note that the bowl of liquid represents the blood of Jesus. The instructions say to write a sin on one of the stones, drop the stone into the blood of Jesus, see the sin symbolically disappear, and know that the blood of Jesus washes clean.

I see two men standing by one of the walls with their hands on each other's shoulders, with heads bowed in prayer. I listen in and hear them forgiving each other of offenses against each other that have resulted in resentment and anger. They are committing to each other and to God to love one another *as God loves them. As I watch, they move to a place set up with a chair, a basin of water, and towels. One man sits in the chair, and the other proceeds to wash his feet. Then they exchange places, and the other washes the feet of the first man. What a visual example this is of the servanthood to which they just committed.*

My attention is drawn back to the table with the communion elements, for there is my pastor kneeling at the table with his father. His arm is across the back and shoulders of his father. Their heads are bowed together, touching. They each hold the communion elements. They are oblivious to everything and everyone else around them. Their countenances are aglow with the joy of the presence of the Lord and each other. I can almost touch the love.

My heart is immensely touched and swells with indescribable emotion because of this visual testimony of peace and love between a father and his son. I remember the relationship with and love between Jesus and His Father. A consuming desire and hunger rises up in me for that kind of relationship with my sons. I pray that there would be a time when I can enter with my sons into the presence of the Lord in communion.

As I experience the privilege of observing this moment, something happens within me; I consider my relationship with and commitment to my pastor. His humbleness in sharing with us, his congregation, and this private moment with his father endears him to my heart and soul. I vow to pray for him and submit to his leadership and authority; somehow I know what I am seeing is representative of Christ's humble relationship with His heavenly Father.

I look around to see where the quiet but audible crying is coming from, and I observe a woman kneeling at a small table and holding something in her hand. I draw closer, and I can clearly see that it is a replica of a large nail that was used to nail Jesus to the cross. She is saying over and over, "Jesus, forgive us. Forgive us. I am so sorry, I am so sorry." Tears come to my eyes also as the shock of the size of that nail and what it was used for penetrate my understanding. I silently join her in asking Jesus to forgive me, and I tell Him I am sorry that my sins caused His suffering.

As I continue to meditate with sorrow on the necessity of the horrible death of Jesus, without which I could not have been saved and redeemed, silence descends on the room, and a lone, plaintive, very beautiful voice sings out, "Were you there when they crucified my Lord, Were you there? O! Sometimes it causes me to tremble, tremble, tremble."[45] I am immediately transported in my mind and soul to the crucifixion. My entire being is consumed with sorrow, but at the same time, there is deep gratitude and thankfulness as I remember what my sin cost my Lord Jesus. I remember what He willingly suffered on my behalf; I remember that "God so loved the world." I eat the bread and drink the wine with a new sense of awareness, and I know that I will never again be able to take communion routinely as a religious ceremony as prescribed by the church.

I sense that the atmosphere in the room is changing, and suddenly a strong, loud male voice calls out, "Hail Jesus, You're my King!"[46] The phrase is echoed loudly by all who are present. He continues, "Your life frees me to sing . . . . I will praise You all my days, . . . Hail Jesus, You're my Lord." He continues through the entire "Victory Chant," and everyone exuberantly echoes each phrase. As the "Victory Chant" comes to a close, everyone gathers in a tight circle, holding hands high, around the communion table; they loudly sing together all the verses of "Crown Him With Many Crowns."[47] The time of communion with the Lord and each other ends with a beautifully harmonized "Amen!" Sorrow is gone, and joy prevails! Great is our Lord, and greatly is He to be praised!

---

[45] American Folk Hymn, author unknown.
[46] Victory Chant, Words and Music by Joseph Vogels, ©Scripture in Song.
[47] Crown Him With Many Crowns, Words by Matthew Bridges and Godfrey Thring. Music by George J. Elvey.

Chapter 18
The Last Session and Afterward

The morning meeting of the last day takes place in the large group and is a time of debriefing where many people share how God touched their lives during their time at the summit.

The communion on the night before was so intense that there is a feeling of being totally separated from "real life." Actually, what has taken place in the last few days is, or should be, real life.

The time at the summit, has progressed to the *Outward* stroke–readiness. This stroke begins with reverence and worship, but it also contains a heavy emphasis on thanksgiving as different people share how God has touched them during this summit. It also is a time for realizing that because God has favored them so greatly, there needs to be a commitment to carry forward, into their lives and ministry at home, the revelations and touch of God experienced at the summit.

There is something that solidifies a commitment, or decision, when it is stated out loud. So, participants should be encouraged to share the commitments they have made and are determined to act upon when they return to their churches, families, and communities. Sometimes, it is appropriate to pray over various people or a group of people, such as those in leadership, laying hands on them and dedicating them to service.

Everyone should be reminded that the purpose of the Prayer Summit was not spiritual self-seeking, nor was it intended for seeking spiritual pleasure. It was not intended to be just an event that ends when people go home, perhaps to wait for the next Prayer Summit.

I am reminded of when the apostles watched Jesus being taken up into Heaven, and even after He was hidden in a cloud. They continued to gaze into Heaven until two men in white appeared beside them and asked, "Men of Galilee, why do you stand gazing up into Heaven?"[48] The implication, of course, was that they had much work to do. As with the apostles, we also have work to do. Let us not stay, gazing and looking back at the Prayer Summit.

The purpose of the Prayer Summit was to seek God, to love Him for who He is, and to continue to do so even in times of suffering and sacrifice, not for what He can give or do. The transformation that has taken place must be nurtured in privacy and in ministry. It must be shared and taught to others. It is not a time to be quarantined because we are contagious. The *"infection"* must spread.

There are many people who are empty and hungry for the incredible love and joy experienced during this time. But they don't know what is causing the emptiness and hunger in their hearts. They don't know what we have learned and experienced at the LCPS.

Pastor Doug from Portland, Oregon, says:

> *How do you know if you are missing something? If you've never known it or experienced it, it's hard to understand. What happens is that when you see, feel, and experience what has been missing, your whole life changes. The change becomes like cool water to a desperate man on a hot day. It quenches your thirst. That's what worship-based prayer did for my soul.*
>
> *For the first half of my ministry, I was a prayerless pastor. Oh, I prayed a few minutes here and there and before meetings. Mostly, I asked God for stuff I needed to make my ministry better; I told God what He ought to do. But my dependence was on my experience, my ability, my hard work, and myself. I couldn't see the deficit, but I knew deep in my soul there was still something missing. There was more to life and ministry than I had yet experienced. I couldn't see it, but I knew it.*
>
> *One day, while I was praying with a group of pastors, one of them invited me to go with him to a Prayer Summit. I resist-*

---

[48] Acts 1:9-11 NKJV

ed because, to me, that meant being transparent about my failed prayer life and the hole in my ministry soul. Somehow, by God's grace, He broke through. I don't know how, nor do I care. I can tell you from the moment of that first session at the Prayer Summit, I instinctively knew that my life would never be the same and that my ministry would forever be changed. I didn't know how to change, but I decided that week that I could never go back to my old ways. I would be willing to do whatever it took to walk this worship-based, soul-empowering, life-transforming journey of prayer with God, and I would take as many people along with me as I could.

My times with God in solitude became rich, and I became even hungrier for spending time with others who shared my heart and God's vision of life-transforming prayer. I wondered how I could introduce this to my people and invite them to share my joy.

Eventually, we packed up 35–40 leaders, staff and other people, and 'infected' them at the Imagine Prayer Conference in Sacramento, California, held by Strategic Renewal International. In the months after the Prayer Conference we developed monthly Fresh Encounters where we worshiped our great God, praised Him, and prayed around a theme. This has become a highlight for many of our people. I continue to grow in my hunger to pray, to care for our community, and to share the grace of Christ with others.

As I look back over this journey, I see some of what was missing. I had a faulty view of God's worthiness, His power, and His desire to love and connect with me. I felt like I had to do the work and ask Him for His blessing. I'm learning that I need to seek Him, pray, wait in dependence on the Holy Spirit, and be obedient to the next step He reveals. I've experienced that trust comes best out of a heart that praises God and offers Him thanksgiving. God can act without my help at all, and His answers can come even when I haven't specifically asked about a particular situation.

I've come to appreciate the fact that personal spiritual renewal and congregational renewal can never come without genuine hearts that are molded and shaped in the refining fire of

> *prayer. Revival and spiritual transformation will never come without the partnership of God's people, who will pray together, care for a community through their servanthood, and share the love stories and love songs of the good news.*
>
> *I think that there are still some things missing, and I'm still thirsty for myself and my people to fall more deeply in love with Jesus. But by God's grace I'm further along on this journey which began when I attended that first Prayer Summit.*

Doug experienced *"infection of his affections"* by attending a Prayer Summit, and if you attend one you will too. Perhaps more important is that by hosting a Prayer Summit you will spread the *"infection"* throughout your congregation, into ministry, and then into the community.

Appendix A
Worship-Based Prayer

There is nothing new about beginning prayer with worship. This is the pattern Jesus gave His disciples in what we call the "Lord's Prayer."[49] What is new to many is the application.

Too many times, worship and prayer are looked upon as two different things, and worship is not the priority. Mark Vroegop says of worship at prayer gatherings in his church, "Worship was the prelude to the 'real' praying, which was requests."

At a Prayer Summit, worship is not only the priority, but it forms the foundation for our prayer. Scripture becomes the frame for our praying. Truly, our prayers become based on worship.

Daniel Henderson teaches a balanced approach to prayer that will not only be effective, but will ignite—set on fire—a congregation with enthusiasm and hunger for seeking God together in prayer. The following is the essence of his teaching. He calls it "worship-based prayer."[50]

---

[49] Matthew 6:9-13
[50] Daniel Henderson with Margaret Saylar, *Fresh Encounters (Nav Press 2004, 2008)* pp 129-133.
Daniel Henderson and Peter Lord, *The 29:59 Plan-Revisioned (Strategic Renewal, 2007)* pp 17-46.

APPENDIX B
THE "4/4 TIME" PATTERN OF PRAYER

The diagram below is patterned after the 4/4 musical beat. It is the motion a director often uses in leading a musical performance. As a prayer tool, it is an effective way by which the Holy Spirit can direct our hearts in a balanced and biblical format of communion with the Lord.

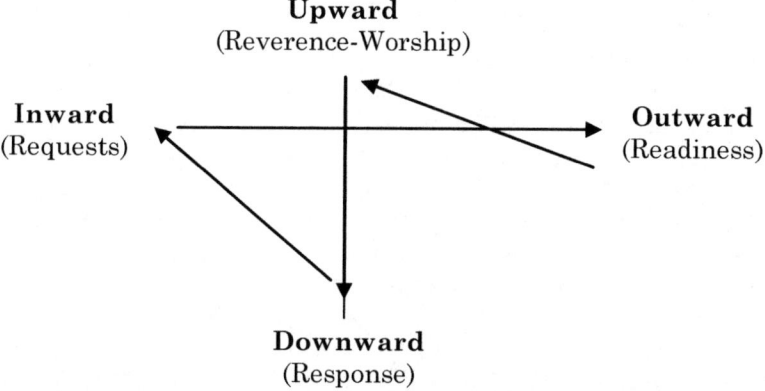

The Upward Stroke: Reverence-Worship

In the prayer pattern Jesus gives His disciples, He urges them to begin with a focus of worship. ("Our Father in Heaven, hallowed be Your Name . . ."[51]) We call this upward focus the "Reverence-Worship" stroke.

In the normal course of prayer ministry, effective prayer is worship-based, not need-based. It begins with the character of God as we take time to focus our entire beings on the wonder of who God is. He is the

---
[51] Matthew 6:9

Father with whom we have a secure, loving relationship through Christ. Yet the Father is in Heaven as sovereign and great God, ruling the world by His might and wisdom. His name (and character) is holy and set apart from everything else in this world.

To enjoy this stroke, do not ask God for anything. Instead, *give* Him the glory and honor due His name in a spirit of biblical and heart-felt worship. To accomplish this, read the Psalms or other portions of Scripture. Revelation 1, 4, and 5; Daniel 9; Nehemiah 9; and 1 Chronicles 29 contain some great thoughts for worship.

Focus on the attributes of God mentioned in these passages. Some commonly available tools used to guide our focus are the names of God, the attributes of God, and the names of Jesus.

Encourage participants to start singing a song of worship as they are led by the Holy Spirit. This will encourage others to praise Him from the heart for who He is, giving His name reverence as they join the singing.

The Downward Stroke: Response

Jesus taught a second element of biblical prayer when He said, "your kingdom come, your will be done on earth as it is in Heaven . . ."[52] This stroke is our response to God's character in prayer. During this stroke, we yield to the control of the Holy Spirit, and we recommit to God's kingdom purposes. Introspection and surrender mark this time of response. Pledge obedience to the will and Word of God, desiring that His perfect will be accomplished in our lives. Confession can be a part of this stroke.

The most practical tool for this stroke is an open Bible. The will of God is the Word of God. The best way to talk to God about His purposes is in His own words. Since you just reverenced the Lord in worship, respond to His character and plan through reciting His Word.

In this time of yielding to the Holy Spirit, someone will read God's holy Word in the holy communion of prayer, that they might fulfill His holy will. Here, someone will often read a passage of Scripture or pray it as God lays it on his or her heart. Many times, after a Scrip-

---

[52] Matthew 6:10

ture passage is read, others spontaneously pray parts of the passage back to God.

The Inward Stoke: Requests

Christ goes on to say, "Give us today our daily bread. Forgive us our debts, as we also forgive our debtors." This is the next element Christ teaches in His model prayer. It involves a period of heartfelt requests, with the themes of provision and purity.

Of course, Jesus had just said that our Father knows our needs before we ask[53]. This is not a time of informing God of our needs as much as it is a conscious trust in God as the perfect definer and provider of our needs. During this stroke, pray about personal requests and the concerns of others. *(At a Prayer Summit, this stroke takes place in the small group gatherings–men with men and women with women.)*

It is important to remember that the Requests stroke follows Reverence-Worship and Response. Only after we have truly worshiped and surrendered our wills to God do we have the proper perspective on our needs.

Not only is God's provision a key concern during this stroke, but so is purity. We commit ourselves to lives of purity and forgiveness as well as living with a clear conscience before God and man. We pledge to seek forgiveness from God, and extend forgiveness to others, daily. Purity is the key to harmony and unity in the body of Christ and must not be neglected in our prayer times with the Lord.

The Outward Stroke: Readiness

While we would love to stay in the posture and pleasure of prayer all day long, we must get off our knees and into the daily battle. The Outward stroke reminds us of the spiritual contest before us and, more importantly, reassures us of the spiritual resources within us.

When we pray, "Lead us not into temptation, but deliver us from the evil one,"[54] we recognize our inability to overcome the temptations and attacks of daily life. We entrust our welfare to the delivering power of our Divine Enabler. This can be done during a time of med-

---

[53] Matthew 6:8
[54] Matthew 6:13

itation and memorization of God's Word, as we gird ourselves with the sword of the Spirit and prepare to counteract personal temptation and spiritual attack.

The Upward Stroke-Reverence

This model of prayer concludes on the same note it began—on a high note of praise. This is like the end of the Lord's Prayer, "For Yours is the Kingdom and the Power and the Glory forever. Amen."[55]

After giving our attention to reverential worship, submissive response, thoughtful requests, spiritual readiness, it is natural to finish with a strong reminder of our awesome God to whom we pray and in whom we trust. His kingdom is unshakable, His power is unmatched, and His glory is unimaginable. Through time spent with Him, we experience a foretaste of His majesty.

As you close this final stroke with songs of praise and declarations of His promises, you will be brought back full circle. (*At a Prayer Summit, this stroke is closed with an extended time of communion where recognition and thanksgiving for the sacrifice and resurrection of Christ is the focus. It is a time of celebration of the new covenant—our blessed hope!*)

---

[55] Matthew 6:13

Appendix C
Sample Outline for Training Worship-Based Prayer Facilitators

PART I

1. The Role of The Prayer Facilitator
2. Desired Qualities in a Prayer Facilitator
3. Understanding Your Authority in Christ
4. The Prayer Facilitator's Personal Preparation Prior to the Summit

PART II

1. Basics of Worship-Based Prayer
2. Praying Scripture vs. Reading Scripture
3. Using a Psalm to Introduce Worship
4. Ways to Encourage Participation
5. Listening to the Holy Spirit
6. Preparing Your Resources
7. Use of Silence
8. Sensitivity to Different Styles of Worship

PART III

1. The Function of the Large Group
2. The Function of the Gender-Specific Small Group
3. Ministering as a Facilitator Team
4. Use of "The Chair"
5. Keeping it Vertical
6. Avoiding Unproductive Words

7. Confronting Hindrances and "Hijackers"
8. Preparing for Spiritual Warfare, both Subtle and Overt, Before, During, and After the Summit

Appendix D
Sample Planning Schedule

Activity	Pre- summit
Find location and sign contract for LCPS	52 weeks before summit
Begin training facilitators	24 weeks before summit
Complete appointment of committee	22 weeks before summit
Full committee begins meeting monthly	20 weeks before summit
Choose Point Facilitator and assistants	16 weeks before summit
Facilitators and assistants begin practice	16 weeks until summit week
Prepare publicity	16 weeks before summit
Prepare registration form	16 weeks before summit
Prepare website for registration	16 weeks before summit
Open registration	12 weeks before summit
Arrangements for the "Seek His Face" Prayer Summit Guide[56]	12 weeks before summit
Reserve church bus	8 weeks before summit
Begin assigning rooms	4 weeks until day of summit
Assemble "Seek His Face" Prayer Summit Guide; pizza party[57]	3 weeks before summit
Discontinue Scholarship applications	2 weeks before summit
Begin printing of nametags	2 weeks until day of summit

---

[56] A book containing material to help the attendees at the summit. It contains instructions and help for worship. See Appendix H.

[57] If you prepare and print your own "Seek His Face" Prayer Summit Guide you may need to assemble it before the summit. This is an activity in which the entire committee participates in and can then share a pizza party together.

Begin assignment of small groups	2 weeks until day of summit
Assemble all supplies	1 week before summit
Assemble attendee packets	1 week before summit
Pre-trip by committee to summit site	Saturday before summit
On-site hospitality team arrival	4-6 hours before summit commences

APPENDIX E
SAMPLE BUDGET

The budget is predicated on the estimated number of people expected to attend the summit. We will use the example of 120 with a breakdown as follows:

94 registered for double occupancy rooms (basic cost including tax and 8 meals)	$139.00
11 registered for single occupancy rooms	$159.00
15 registered for quad occupancy	$120.00
Using this example, the **site billing** would be:	**$16,615.00**

Estimated Expenses:

Communion	$25.00
Miscellaneous	$50.00
Name tags	$120.00
Postage	$25.00
Publicity	$320.00
Refreshments	$120.00
Scholarships (4 at $50.00 each)	$200.00
"Seek His Face" Prayer Summit Guide	$350.00
Supplies	$50.00
Pastor Registration	$140.00
Spouse	$140.00
Babysitting	$200.00
Total Expenses:	**$1,740.00**

Total Summit Cost: $18,355.00

Divide the Total Expense of $1,740.00 by 120 (estimated attendance) for a total of $15.00 per person.

Final cost: (per person)

Basic cost: $139.00 Double Occupancy + $15.00	$154.00
$159.00 Single Occupancy + $15.00	$174.00
$120.00 Quad Occupancy + $15.00	$135.00
Total income from registration fees:	**$18,415.00**
Profit or (loss)	*$60.00*

APPENDIX F
PRAYER SUMMIT DESCRIPTION AND GUIDELINES

The Prayer Summit is a gathering of Christians who will spend several days seeking the Lord and His agenda for their individual lives, families, churches, and communities. It is a gathering of individuals who take seriously their responsibility to corporately prepare their lives and churches for an outpouring of God's blessing. **But it is much more!**

It is an unprecedented group and individual experience of the glory of Christ within and among His people.

It is a prolonged praise and prayer meeting at which individuals will discover and express their oneness in Christ.

- It is an environment where personal revival is nurtured and common.
- It is a time for repentance and reconciliation.
- It is a time of spiritual warfare as Christians are led to deal with areas of personal and corporate sin.
- It can be the beginning of a new expressed dependence on God, both personally and in the church, and may be the first phase of real revival.

OUR FOCUS IS TO DO THE FOLLOWING:

- Seek God's face more than His hand (that is, who He is and His character, not His works).
- Passionately seek to understand, know, and intimately relate to Him, first and foremost.

- Talk to Him, not just about Him.
- Sing to Him, not just about Him.

Anything else will only be significant if it is in response to these focal points. As we experience His heart through this extended time of worship and devotion, we can then respond to His will as His Spirit directs.

We come with no group or personal Agendas,
And we will leave with only one----
His!

GROUP DYNAMICS

- *Large group meetings* – will be held in the main room and will include everyone.
- *Small groups* – will be utilized allowing opportunity for more intimate interaction and prayer.
- *Personal time* – will be encouraged as the Lord leads.
- *Code of Silence* – will be used as the Lord directs.
  (*Note*: A Code of Silence is a time specified by a facilitator, in response to the Holy Spirit's leading, during which there is to be no talking–conversation or communication. The time is to be spent in silent meditation with the Lord.)
- *Communion time* – one or more times will be celebrated.

FORMAT
We will utilize four basic components.

- **Prayer**
  Early in the summit, we will strongly focus on praise and worship. Later on, as the Spirit leads, we will enter into other dimensions of prayer (confession, surrender, etc.). You will be encouraged to pray privately at all times and publicly only as the Spirit clearly directs your heart, in a way that will edify God and the participants.

- **Singing**
  Spontaneous songs of praise and worship will be encouraged throughout the summit. All singing will be done ***a cappella*** throughout the summit. Hymnals and songbooks are available for those who need the words, but these tools are not to

be the focus. You are encouraged to sing wholeheartedly to the Lord in blended harmony with other voices.

- **Scripture Reading**
  The inclusion of Scripture is vital to our encounter, since we are here to hear from God. You may read a passage of scripture aloud at any time during which the Spirit of God directs it. If you would like to make it a responsive reading, begin your portion by saying loudly, **"It is written . . ."** This will be our cue to repeat the phrases of His Word aloud.

- **Personal Response**
  As the Lord directs, we will encourage some times of personal response as a part of the summit flow. This will become a more prominent part of the summit in the last couple of days, especially in the smaller groups. Your response should focus on how God has revealed Himself to you and how you are being prompted to respond to Him in obedience to His Word.

There will be a primary facilitator for the large group and one for each of the small groups. A listening and facilitating team will assist the primary facilitators in sensing the Lord's direction, and in bringing focus to the large group and the small groups.

The listening and facilitating teams will be introduced to you. You are encouraged to give input and feedback to any of these individuals as the summit progresses. They will be meeting regularly with the facilitator to discuss the progress of the summit.

Additionally, other people are responsible for overseeing the many administrative details. All setup and registration questions should be directed to them.

GUIDELINES

- **Sensitivity is Essential!**
  This is not a hymn-singing time where everyone picks his or her favorite song. Neither is it a session for individuals to read their favorite verses. Finally, we are not here to rehearse prepared prayer lists.

LET HIM WHO HAS EARS HEAR
WHAT THE SPIRIT IS SAYING TO THE CHURCH!!

- **Continuity is Important.**
  As you share publicly, be sure you are led of the Spirit. Because He is a God of order, we believe your sharing should be consistent with the particular area(s) of focus in which we are being directed at any given time. When you share, please do so loudly enough that all may hear and be edified.

- **A Variety of Expressions are Encouraged.**
  Some will choose to sit, and some will kneel. Others may stand, walk, or lay prostrate. Some will sing and worship with eyes opened, others with eyes closed. Some may pray lifting their hands; some will not. Our focus is on God, not one another. Because we want this singular focus to be very intense, we encourage participants to use whatever "forms" will best help them focus on the Lord.

- **Silence is Acceptable.**
  There may be times when no one is led to pray, sing, or read out loud. Please respect that silence. We would rather have Spirit-led quietness than someone talking just to break an uncomfortable silence. ***"Be still and know that I am God,"*** says the Lord.

- **Listening is Vital.**
  We must hear the Lord's voice through His Word and by His Spirit. Listening to the directions of the facilitators will be important for the sake of unity in focus and direction. Listening to others as they share will prompt your own heart as the Lord speaks through them.

  ***CONFIDENTIALITY IS ABSOLUTELY NECESSARY!

  What you hear must stay within the group and not ever leave it. That includes not sharing anything you hear as a prayer request or in some other setting.

Appendix G
Sample Prayer Summit Schedule

- Although we do not have an agenda, we do have a schedule. It is expected, barring illness that you will attend all sessions.
- Please fast from all phone use during the summit, leaving cell phones in your car or another safe place. Emergency Phone is:_____
- Registration will not be accepted after 8:00 a.m. Thursday.

WEDNESDAY:
First Session -- 7:30 p.m.

THURSDAY:
Breakfast -- 8:00 a.m.
First Session -- 9:15 a.m.
Lunch --- 12:15 p.m.
Facilitator Meeting -- 1:00 p.m.
Second Session --- 1:30 p.m.
Dinner -- 5:30 p.m.
Facilitator Meeting -- 6:30 p.m.
Third Session --- 7:00 p.m.

FRIDAY:
Breakfast -- 8:00 a.m.
Facilitator Meeting -- 8:45 a.m.
First Session -- 9:15 a.m.
Lunch --- 12:15 p.m.
Facilitator Meeting -- 1:00 p.m.
Second Session --- 1:30 p.m.

Dinner .... 6:00 p.m.
Facilitator Meeting .... 7:00 p.m.
Third Session .... 7:30 p.m.

SATURDAY:
Breakfast .... 8:00 a.m.
Facilitator Meeting .... 8:45 a.m.
Final Session .... 9:15 a.m.
Lunch .... 12:30 p.m.
DISMISS: .... 2:00 p.m.

APPENDIX H
THE "SEEK HIS FACE" PRAYER SUMMIT GUIDE SONG (CHORUS) BOOK AND PRAYER STATIONS

THE "SEEK HIS FACE" PRAYER SUMMIT GUIDE

The focus of the Local Church Prayer Summit is on God, who He is, and His character. Since many people have little or no experience in concentrating on God's character or attributes, it is a great help to provide them with some material that will guide them both during the summit and in their personal time when they go home. This material should include God's character in His manifestation as God, Jesus, and the Holy Spirit, since His working in our lives and creation is different in each of the three persons of the Trinity.

It gives a feeling of security and encourages participation when people have some material to help them in Spirit-led, worship-based prayer, especially if this is their first exposure. Therefore, the inclusion of Scripture passages, thoughts on prayer and worship, pattern prayers, and guides to self-examination are desirable.

Keep the format of this book within the "4/4 Time" prayer pattern.

The first section should concentrate on Reverence/Worship: the *Upward* stroke. Include in this section the names of God, names of Jesus, and names of the Holy Spirit. Include thoughts on worship and prayer as well as appropriate Scripture passages. This section is the most important and should make up one half of the book.

The next section should include material to aid in response to God's character: who He is. This is the *Downward* stroke. Thoughts and

Scripture passages on His holiness, faith, and trust as well as listening and silence are placed in this section.

The following section is petition and intercession: the *Inward* stroke. Items on forgiveness, pride, fear, submission, bitterness, and salvation should be included here. Remember that in this context, petition and intercession is not for others, but for oneself. Pattern prayers of forgiveness (both giving forgiveness and asking God for forgiveness) and salvation should be included.

The material for the *Outward* stroke should include Scripture passages and material related to a grateful heart and thanksgiving. Material relating to the armor of God, His protection, and His provision are appropriate here.

Above all, remember that this book is about worshiping God and is not a venue to include favorite writings or a place to promote one's own thoughts. Most of the book should be about God, not what *people* have written or think. Include in the book the summit guidelines, pages for journaling, and the schedule for easy reference.

Note: *If you would prefer, contact Strategic Renewal International (www.strategicrenewal.com) for the "Seek His Face" Prayer Summit Guide.*

THE SONG (CHORUS) BOOK

One of the components of worship at a LCPS is singing. Not everyone can or has memorized the words to worship choruses or hymns that will be sung; yet, a good share of the worship will be in this form. Therefore, it is necessary to provide some kind of booklet with the words to songs or choruses that will likely be used at the summit. Using a booklet is suggested as opposed to loose papers. Booklets allow you to provide a variety of songs and are easier to navigate when searching for songs. You can prepare your own book of material, or you can take an existing chorus book and provide a new table of contents. **Be sure you comply with all copyright laws.**

At a Prayer Summit, there is not a calling out of the number of the song to be sung; rather, the song is just started by someone. Thus, people often find it very difficult to locate the song in their book. The most efficient way to solve this problem is to list the songs alphabetically, giving the page number of the first line of each song. That way, everyone can quickly find the song without knowing its exact title. Regardless of the way you provide the material, it should be referenced in this way.

PRAYER STATIONS

The most efficient learning takes place when we use as many of the five senses as we can. It has been said that the gateway, or entry, into the soul and spirit is through the five senses. Prayer Stations are designed to use all of our senses to enable us to experience God's presence in many different ways.

Prayer Stations were introduced into the adult community of our church by our Youth Pastor, Tom Ramsay, who said, "I have been surprised to see even men walk out of this experience with tears streaming down their faces."

And, indeed, so have I.

Each station is designed to have a different impact. The kind of Prayer Station you can create is limited only by your imagination. However, they do have some common elements. Each one is a small oasis by itself. Some need a small table, a card table, TV tray, or a small end table. Some need kneeling cushions, while some need a chair. They all need some kind of lighting. If you use candles, do not leave them unattended. Semi-darkness is needed for effect. Do not place the stations too close to each other. Allow for some privacy. Most stations should have a supply of Kleenex nearby.

Each station will need to have instructions on how to use it. This is done by printing, as briefly as possible, an explanation on an 8 1/2" x 11 piece of stiff white cardboard. It is wise to laminate this sign with a plastic coating. The signs are then placed upright on the table or floor next to the station. Plate holders or frames, which can be bought at most craft stores, are useful for this.

A cross is very helpful, as well. Use two 4 x 4's and a sturdy stand. Drape a purple cloth over the arms and perhaps thorns on the top. Provide nails and a hammer, along with paper and pencils for writing sins and burdens, so that attendees can nail the written notes to the cross.

Several Prayer Stations are described in the Communion chapter as ideas to get you started.

RESOURCES

To request information or additional summit materials, purchase resources, or request Daniel Henderson to speak at an event, visit Strategic Renewal International at www.strategicrenewal.com. Information on hosting a Local Church Prayer Summit is also available through International Renewal Ministries at www.prayersummits.net.

Joe Aldrich, *Reunitus: Building Bridges to Each Other through Prayer Summits (1992* Multnomah Press, 10209 SE Division Street Portland Oregon 97266). Available at www.prayersummits.net.

Daniel Henderson, *PRAYzing: Creative prayer experiences from A to Z* (2007 NavPress P.O. Box 35001 Colorado Sprints, Co 80935).

Daniel Henderson & Peter Lord, *The 29:59 Plan-Revisioned* (2007 Strategic Renewal International, www.strategicrenewal.com)

Daniel Henderson with Margaret Saylar, *Fresh Encounters: Experiencing Transformation through United Worship-Based Prayer* (2004 NavPress P.O. Box 35004 Colorado Springs, Co. 80935).

T.C. Horton, *The Wonderful Names of Our Wonderful Lord, 365 Names and Titles of the Lord Jesus Christ found in the Old and New Testaments* (1996, Barbour and Company Inc. {P.O. Box 719 Uhrichsville, Ohio 44683).

James L. Nicodem, *250 of God's Attributes* www.ccclife.org/story.asp?storyid=720.

Ann Spangler, *Praying the Names of God* (2004 Zondervan, Grand Rapids Michigan 49530).

Elmer L. Towns, *The Names of the Holy Spirit* (1994 Regal/Gospel Light 1-800-4 GOSPEL).

Elmer L. Towns & Daniel Henderson, *The Church that Prays Together, Inside the Life of 10 Dynamic Churches* (2008 NavPress P.O. Box 35004 Colorado Springs Co. 80935, www.NavPress.com)

Check out these other empowering resources
from strategic**renewal**

Wake Up and Pray Group Study

God is not the author of boredom, especially when we are conversing with Him. Ignite new creativity and excitement in your prayer life through this dynamic six-week DVD series, used in conjunction with the *Wake Up and Pray* workbook and the book, *PRAYzing: Creative Prayer Experiences from A to Z.* Available in DVD or digital download formats at www.strategicrenewal.com

The Digital 29:59 Plan: A Guide To Communion With God

Since it's development over 30 years ago, the 29:59 Plan has sold over 600,00 copies and has impacted the lives of countless believers. This timeless resource is now available in an updated format. The digital 29:59 Plan will not only teach you how to spend time with God, but with this new web-based format, it will allow you to do so in a way that is totally customized to fit your lifestyle. Start your free 7-day trial membership at www.pray2959.com

The Power To Change Group Study

Jesus Christ transforms lives! When you experience the profound difference of God-focused, worship-based prayer, your faith and life will never be the same. Used in conjunction with the book, *Transforming Prayer*, this five-week study includes group leaders guides, workbooks for group discussion, and guides for interactive prayer. Available in DVD or digital download format at www.strategicrenewal.com

Igniting the Heart of the Church

strategic**renewal**